SIGNS FROM THE SOUTH

THE CHARITY LEAGUE, INC., OF BIRMINGHAM, ALABAMA

SIGNS FROM THE SOUTH

Published by
The Charity League, Inc.

Copyright © 2007 by

The Charity League, Inc.
P.O. Box 530233
Birmingham, Alabama 35253
www.TheCharityLeague.org

This cookbook is a collection of favorite recipes,
which are not necessarily original recipes.

All rights reserved. No part of this publication may be reproduced
in any form or by any means, electronic or mechanical, including
photocopying and recording, or by any information storage or
retrieval system, without prior written permission from
The Charity League, Inc.
ISBN-10: 0-9779430-0-3
ISBN-13: 978-0-9779430-0-5

Edited, Designed, and Manufactured by

CommunityClassics™

An imprint of

FRP™

P. O. Box 305142
Nashville, Tennessee 37230
800-358-0560

Manufactured in China
First Printing: 2007
3,000 copies

ACKNOWLEDGMENTS

As the old saying goes, "When life gives you lemons . . . make lemonade!" Many children are born with or develop hearing and speech impairments. The Charity League, Inc., of Birmingham, Alabama, serves to make this lemonade a bit sweeter.

Many hours of diligent hard work were put into this unique collection of recipes. With the purpose of raising a greater awareness of the organization, *Signs from the South* will allow you to explore and savor the many styles of cooking from an extraordinary group of women. With a touch of southern hospitality, each recipe will entice your senses.

ABOUT THE COVER

Thank you to the wonderful children at E.P.I.C. for allowing us to use their hands for the cover. Their hearts are filled with genuine gratitude every time we step into the school building. The smiles and hugs bring a special warmth that is untouchable.

The cover "Hands" belong to:
Kymyana Showers, Denireata Hasberry, Ke'Ariel Rice, Jazzlyn Mann, Ashley Laster, Eddie Thomas and Steven Lambert.

ABOUT THE CHARITY LEAGUE, INC.

The Charity League, Inc., is a nonprofit service organization of approximately one hundred women committed to serving the hearing- and speech-impaired children of Alabama through both volunteer hours and financial support. Since its formation in 1959, The Charity League has succeeded in providing more than 171,000 volunteer hours and has raised in excess of $2 million for various worthwhile endeavors. **One hundred percent of all proceeds are used to benefit the special children it serves.** Support for the children is achieved through many outlets.

The Charity League Hearing and Speech Center, located at Children's Hospital in Birmingham, Alabama, is a program close to the hearts of families with hearing- and speech-impaired children. Many children have received funding for their cochlear implants through the HEAR (Hearing Enrichment Assessment and Research) Center. Scholarships are granted for those patients in need of speech or language therapy, and funding is provided for families needing assistance with purchasing hearing aids. Additional funds are put to use for Parent Support Programs, Parent Library, and a preschool program at the Center. Throughout each calendar year, funds are set aside for needed equipment for the Center, such as computer software, digital hearing aids, therapy materials, and much more. The League provides volunteer assistance to the staff of the Hearing and Speech Center, and sponsors parent forums on speech and language development in conjunction with speech/language pathologists and audiologists from Children's Health System.

E.P.I.C. (Educational Program for the Individual Child), a public school in the Birmingham City School System, specializes in the education of exceptional children. Funding is provided to purchase phonic ear equipment, ear molds, transducers, and speech trainers to name a few. MANY volunteer hours are served working with the hearing- and speech-impaired children attending E.P.I.C. through such programs as arts and crafts, creative movement, and perceptual motor and speech pathology.

Many other services to the community are provided to smaller but much needed programs. Volunteer assistance is given for hearing and speech screenings for kindergarten children throughout Jefferson and Shelby counties in Alabama. There is a "Visit to the Hospital" program at Children's Hospital in Birmingham, Alabama, that provides tours of the One-Day Surgery Center for groups of kindergarten and grade-school children in the public school systems.

The Charity League plans and organizes a booth at "The Market," where all proceeds benefit a special request for a hearing- and speech-impaired child in the state of Alabama. Also, the ladies participate in "The Gala" fund-raiser for Children's Hospital by decorating a large tree in Birmingham, Alabama.

A "Special Request Fund" was established in 1994 to assist schools in purchasing needed equipment. The fund has been used in both Jefferson and Shelby county, as well as in communities in South America. Since 2002, we have granted funding for hearing- and speech-impaired children in more than sixty schools.

The "Swing Fore Scholarships" Golf Tournament was established in 2002 to provide aid to a hearing- or speech-impaired college student in Alabama. This scholarship program has increased each year with applicants striving to attend college and receive an education with the help of these funds. For an application and more information, please see our Web site at www.TheCharityLeague.org.

Beginning in 2005, the Annual Fund-raising Drive concentrated our fund-raising efforts on individual and corporate support. Our sole financial support is from the community. We want to ensure that the hearing- and speech-impaired children of Alabama will continue to receive the support they need. Anyone can contribute and join us to make a difference in these children's lives.

And our newest endeavor, *Signs from the South*, will increase funds to financially support our programs. All proceeds will benefit the hearing- and speech-impaired children of Alabama. We strive to make a difference in these children's lives every day. Whether it is through an implant, literature, or even a computer program, the assistance we provide these children, and their families, schools, and hospitals will change their paths in life forever. Thank you for helping us make a difference.

TABLE OF CONTENTS

APPETIZERS, BREADS & BEVERAGES 7

SOUPS, SALADS & SANDWICHES 31

VEGETABLES & SIDE DISHES 57

MAIN DISHES 81

DESSERTS 115

APPETIZERS BREADS & BEVERAGES

APPETIZERS, BREADS & BEVERAGES

BACON CHEESE CUPS

6 ounces cream cheese, softened
1 egg
2 tablespoons milk
1/2 cup (2 ounces) shredded Swiss cheese
1 green onion, chopped
1 (10-count) can refrigerator flaky biscuits
5 slices bacon, crisp-cooked and crumbled

Beat the cream cheese, egg and milk in a bowl with an electric mixer at medium speed to mix well. Stir in the Swiss cheese and green onion. Separate the biscuits and pat each into a 5-inch circle on a work surface. Press the dough into greased muffin cups, leaving a 1/4-inch rim at the top. Sprinkle half the bacon equally over the bottom of the cups. Spoon 2 tablespoons of the cheese mixture into each cup. Bake at 375 degrees for 22 minutes or until set. Sprinkle the remaining bacon equally over the tops of the bacon cheese cups and press gently. Serves 10.

KATHY TYNER, *Senior Sustainer*

APPETIZERS, BREADS & BEVERAGES

WALNUT AND BLUE CHEESE BITES

1 1/2 cups all-purpose flour
2 to 3 tablespoons cracked pepper
8 ounces blue cheese
1/4 cup (1/2 stick) butter
1 cup chopped walnuts
2 egg yolks, lightly beaten

Combine the flour and pepper in a bowl and mix well. Cut in the cheese and butter with a pastry blender or fork until crumbly. Add the walnuts and egg yolks and mix well. Shape into a ball. Knead on a floured work surface until well mixed. Divide the dough in half and shape each half into a log. Wrap each log in plastic wrap and chill for 2 hours. Cut the logs into 1/4-inch slices and place on an ungreased baking sheet. Bake at 425 degrees for 8 to 10 minutes or until golden brown. Remove the slices to a wire rack to cool. Serve warm or at room temperature. Store in an airtight container in the refrigerator for up to 1 week. Makes 6 dozen slices.

DINA MANLY

APPETIZERS, BREADS & BEVERAGES

SALMON LOG

1 (16-ounce) can salmon, drained and flaked
8 ounces cream cheese, softened
1 tablespoon lemon juice
1 teaspoon horseradish
2 teaspoons grated onion
1 teaspoon liquid smoke
1/4 teaspoon salt
1/2 cup chopped nuts

Combine the salmon, cream cheese, lemon juice, horseradish, onion, liquid smoke and salt in a bowl and mix well. Chill, covered, for 3 hours or longer. Shape into a log and wrap in plastic wrap. Chill for 2 to 3 hours. Spread the nuts over waxed paper. Roll the log in the nuts. Chill, covered, until ready to serve. Serve with crackers. Serves 32.

TERI HIBBARD, *President 2006–2007*

APPETIZERS, BREADS & BEVERAGES

TEMPTING CHEESE BALL

8 ounces cream cheese, softened
1 bunch green onions, chopped
1 (2-ounce) jar dried beef, finely chopped
1 (2-ounce) package chopped nuts

Combine the cream cheese, green onions and dried beef in a bowl. Mix with your hands and shape into a ball. Roll in the nuts spread over waxed paper. Chill, covered, until ready to serve. Serve with your favorite party crackers. Serves 12 to 16.

SANDY VINES

APPETIZERS, BREADS & BEVERAGES

MEXICAN PIZZA

8 ounces cream cheese, softened
1 (19-ounce) can chili with beans
2 (4-ounce) cans diced green chiles
3/4 cup chopped scallions
2 cups (8 ounces) shredded Mexican-blend cheese
2 (3-ounce) cans sliced black olives, drained
1 (13-ounce) package tortilla chips

Spread the cream cheese over the bottom of a 9x12-inch baking dish. Spread the chili over the cream cheese. Sprinkle with the green chiles and scallions. Top with the Mexican-blend cheese and sprinkle with the olives. Bake at 400 degrees for 20 minutes or until the cheese is bubbly. Serve with the tortilla chips. Serves 32.

NOTE: *Do not use fat-free or light cream cheese in this recipe.*

MARY KAY CAMPBELL

APPETIZERS, BREADS & BEVERAGES

DRIED BEEF DIP

8 ounces cream cheese, softened
2 tablespoons milk
1 (2-ounce) jar dried beef, chopped
1/4 cup chopped bell pepper
2 tablespoons dried onion flakes
1/2 teaspoon pepper
1/2 cup sour cream
1/2 cup chopped pecans
2 tablespoons butter
1/2 teaspoon salt

Combine the cream cheese, milk, dried beef, bell pepper, onion flakes and pepper in a bowl and mix well. Fold in the sour cream. Spoon into a baking dish. Sauté the pecans in the butter and salt in a small skillet over medium heat until the pecans are toasted. Sprinkle over the cream cheese mixture. Bake at 350 degrees for 20 minutes. Serve with crackers or chips. Serves 20.

ASHLEY HIBBARD

HOT BACON AND SWISS DIP

8 ounces cream cheese, softened
1/2 cup mayonnaise
2 tablespoons chopped green onions
1 cup (4 ounces) shredded Swiss cheese
8 slices bacon, crisp-cooked and crumbled
Butter crackers, crushed

Combine the cream cheese, mayonnaise, green onions and Swiss cheese in a bowl and mix well. Spoon into a baking dish. Sprinkle with the bacon and cracker crumbs. Bake at 350 degrees for 20 minutes. Serve with butter crackers. Serves 32.

JULIE WOODSON

APPETIZERS, BREADS & BEVERAGES

BIRMINGHAM SIN

1 (5-ounce) can chunk ham, drained and flaked
1 cup sour cream
8 ounces cream cheese, softened
2 cups (8 ounces) shredded Cheddar cheese
1 teaspoon Worcestershire sauce
3 to 5 green onions, chopped
1 loaf French bread

Combine the ham, sour cream, cream cheese, Cheddar cheese, Worcestershire sauce and half the green onions in a bowl and mix well. Hollow out the bread leaving a 1-inch-thick wall. Cut the removed bread into cubes and toast, if desired. Spoon the ham mixture into the hollowed bread. Sprinkle with the remaining green onions. Place on a baking sheet. Bake at 325 degrees for 25 to 35 minutes or until bubbly and light brown. Serve with the toasted bread, corn chips or crackers. Serves 32.

DONNA CONKLIN

APPETIZERS, BREADS & BEVERAGES

SAUSAGE CHEESE DIP

1 pound bulk pork sausage, cooked and drained
8 ounces cream cheese, softened
4 cups (16 ounces) shredded Cheddar cheese
1 cup sour cream
2 (4-ounce) cans diced green chiles
1 round loaf Hawaiian bread
1 (10-ounce) package corn chips

Combine the sausage, cream cheese, Cheddar cheese, sour cream and green chiles in a bowl and mix well. Hollow out the bread leaving a 1-inch-thick wall. Spoon the sausage mixture into the hollowed bread. Place on a baking sheet. Bake at 350 degrees for 1 hour or until the cheese is bubbly. Serve surrounded by the corn chips. Serves 40.

BRANDI YAGHMAI

APPETIZERS, BREADS & BEVERAGES

HOT CRAB DIP

8 ounces cream cheese, softened
2 (6-ounce) cans crab meat, drained
3/4 cup mayonnaise
1/4 cup (1 ounce) grated Parmesan cheese
3/4 cup (3 ounces) shredded Cheddar cheese
2 tablespoons finely chopped onion
1 tablespoon lemon juice
1 teaspoon Worcestershire sauce
Hot red pepper sauce to taste
Garlic salt to taste

Beat the cream cheese in a bowl until light and fluffy. Add the crab meat, mayonnaise, Parmesan cheese, Cheddar cheese, onion, lemon juice, Worcestershire sauce, hot sauce and garlic salt and mix well. Spoon into an 8×8-inch baking dish. Bake at 375 degrees for 10 to 15 minutes or until bubbly. Serves 24.

NIKKI HARKINS, *President 2002–2003*

APPETIZERS, BREADS & BEVERAGES

HOT FETA ARTICHOKE DIP

2 (14-ounce) cans artichoke hearts, drained and chopped
2 (8-ounce) packages traditional feta cheese, crumbled
1 1/2 cups mayonnaise
1 cup (4 ounces) shredded Parmesan cheese
1 (2-ounce) jar diced pimentos, drained (optional)
1 tablespoon minced garlic

Combine the artichokes, feta cheese, mayonnaise, Parmesan cheese, pimentos and garlic in a bowl and mix well. Spoon into a baking dish. Bake at 350 degrees for 45 minutes or until light brown. Serve with crackers or corn chips. Serves 40.

LORI HADLEY

APPETIZERS, BREADS & BEVERAGES

CORN DIP

2 (11-ounce) cans Mexicorn, drained
2 cups (8 ounces) shredded Cheddar cheese
2/3 cup sour cream
1/3 cup mayonnaise
Chopped green onions to taste
Chopped jalapeño chiles to taste

Combine the corn, cheese, sour cream, mayonnaise, green onions and jalapeños in a bowl and mix well. Chill, covered, until ready to serve. Serves 32.

DEBBIE SELF

"CORNY" CHEESE DIP

1 (7-ounce) can Mexicorn, drained
2 cups (8 ounces) shredded sharp Cheddar cheese
1/2 cup sour cream
1/2 cup mayonnaise
1/4 to 1/2 cup chopped green onions
1/2 teaspoon salt
1 teaspoon chopped fresh cilantro, or to taste

Combine the corn, cheese, sour cream, mayonnaise, green onions, salt and cilantro in a bowl and mix well. Chill, covered, until cold. Serve with crackers, corn chips or fresh vegetables. Serves 24.

ELLEN SHUFFLEBARGER, *Senior Sustainer*

APPETIZERS, BREADS & BEVERAGES

THE BEST GUACAMOLE

2 small avocados
1/2 white onion, chopped
1 large or 2 small tomatoes, chopped
1 garlic clove, pressed
Juice of 1/2 lemon or lime
3 dashes of hot red pepper sauce
1/2 teaspoon cumin
Salt and pepper to taste

Mash the avocados in a bowl with a fork. Stir briskly with a spoon until the avocados are creamy. Add the onion, tomato, garlic and lemon juice and mix well. Stir in the hot sauce, cumin, salt and pepper. Serves 18.

ALEXANDRA ALLYN

VIDALIA ONION DIP

3 large Vidalia onions, chopped
2 tablespoons butter
1 cup mayonnaise
2 cups (8 ounces) shredded sharp Cheddar cheese
1/2 teaspoon Tabasco sauce
1 garlic clove, minced

Sauté the onions in the butter in a skillet over medium heat until tender. Remove from the heat. Add the mayonnaise, cheese, Tabasco sauce and garlic and mix well. Spoon into a buttered baking dish. Bake at 350 degrees for 25 minutes. Serve with tortilla chips, corn chips or crackers. Serves 32.

LISA BOLAND

APPETIZERS, BREADS & BEVERAGES

HOT SPINACH DIP

1 (10-ounce) package frozen chopped spinach, thawed and drained
2 cups (8 ounces) shredded Monterey Jack cheese
8 ounces cream cheese, softened
1 (10-ounce) can tomatoes with green chiles
1/3 cup half-and-half
1/4 cup (1 ounce) grated Parmesan cheese
2 to 3 tablespoons chopped jalapeño chiles

Combine the spinach, Monterey Jack cheese, cream cheese, tomatoes with green chiles, half-and-half, Parmesan cheese and jalapeños in a bowl and mix well. Spoon into a baking dish. Bake at 400 degrees for 20 to 25 minutes. Serve with tortilla chips. Serves 32.

STACEY REED

BLACK BEAN SALSA

1 (15-ounce) can black beans, drained
1 (11-ounce) can Shoe Peg corn, drained
4 to 6 ounces feta cheese, crumbled
4 green onions, chopped
1/2 cup olive oil
1/2 cup apple cider vinegar
1/2 cup sugar

Combine the black beans, corn, cheese and green onions in a bowl and mix well. Whisk the olive oil, vinegar and sugar in a bowl. Pour over the bean mixture and mix well. Chill, covered, until cold. Serve with corn chips. Serves 32.

GINNY CAMPBELL

APPETIZERS, BREADS & BEVERAGES

BANANA BUTTERSCOTCH BREAD

1 cup mashed bananas
3/4 cup sugar
2 eggs
1/4 cup (1/2 stick) butter, melted
1 3/4 cups all-purpose flour
2 teaspoons baking powder
1/2 teaspoon baking soda
1/2 teaspoon salt
1 teaspoon ground cinnamon
1/4 cup milk
1 cup (6 ounces) butterscotch chips
2/3 cup chopped nuts
1/3 cup chopped nuts

Combine the bananas, sugar, eggs and melted butter in a bowl and mix well. Combine the flour, baking powder, baking soda, salt and cinnamon in a large bowl and mix well. Beat in the banana mixture alternately with the milk with an electric mixer and beat well. Stir in the butterscotch chips and 2/3 cup nuts. Line the bottom of a 5x9-inch loaf pan with waxed paper. Grease the waxed paper and sides of the pan. Spoon the batter into the prepared pan. Sprinkle with 1/3 cup nuts. Bake at 350 degrees for 1 hour and 20 minutes or until the bread tests done. Cool in the pan for 10 minutes. Remove to a wire rack and let cool for 20 minutes before serving. Serves 12.

RENEE W. BOOKER, *President 1994–1995*

APPETIZERS, BREADS & BEVERAGES

CRANBERRY BREAD

2 cups all-purpose flour
1 cup sugar
1 1/2 teaspoons baking powder
1 teaspoon baking soda
1 teaspoon salt
1/3 cup orange juice
2 tablespoons vegetable oil
1 egg, beaten
1 cup fresh cranberries

Sift the flour, sugar, baking powder, baking soda and salt together. Mix the orange juice and oil in a large bowl. Add the egg and mix well. Add the dry ingredients and mix well. Fold in the cranberries. Spoon into a greased 5×9-inch loaf. Bake at 350 degrees for 1 hour or until a wooden pick inserted in the center comes out clean. Cool in the pan for 10 minutes. Remove to a wire rack to cool completely. Serves 12.

NOTE: *You may make two smaller loaves instead of one large loaf. Reduce the baking time if making two smaller loaves.*

PATTI JENSEN, *Senior Sustainer*

APPETIZERS, BREADS & BEVERAGES

HOLIDAY PUMPKIN BREAD

3 cups sugar
1 cup olive oil
4 eggs, beaten
1 (15-ounce) can pumpkin
3 cups all-purpose flour
2 teaspoons baking soda
1 1/2 teaspoons salt
1 to 2 teaspoons ground cinnamon
1 teaspoon nutmeg
2/3 cup water

Combine the sugar, olive oil, eggs and pumpkin in a bowl and mix well. Stir in the flour, baking soda, salt, cinnamon and nutmeg. Add the water and mix well. Pour into four greased 3 3/4×7 1/2-inch loaf pans. Bake at 350 degrees for 1 hour or until the bread tests done. Cool in the pans for 10 minutes. Remove to a wire rack to cool completely. Serves 24.

VALLIE PATE, *Senior Sustainer*

APPETIZERS, BREADS & BEVERAGES

PECAN PIE MUFFINS

1 cup packed dark brown sugar
1/2 cup all-purpose flour
1 cup chopped pecans
10 2/3 tablespoons butter, melted and cooled
2 eggs beaten

Combine the brown sugar, flour and pecans in a bowl and mix well. Combine the melted butter and eggs in a bowl and mix well. Add to the pecan mixture and stir just until combined. Fill miniature muffin cups coated with nonstick cooking spray 2/3 full. Bake at 350 degrees for 20 to 25 minutes. Cool in the pan for 5 minutes. Remove to a wire rack to cool completely. Makes 18 miniature muffins.

ROBIN RICH

APPETIZERS, BREADS & BEVERAGES

SOUTHERN CORN BREAD

1 tablespoon bacon drippings
1 1/2 cups buttermilk
1 egg, beaten
1 teaspoon salt
2 teaspoons baking powder
1/4 teaspoon baking soda
2 cups cornmeal

Melt the bacon drippings in a 10-inch cast-iron skillet in a 450-degree oven. Combine the buttermilk, egg, salt, baking powder, baking soda and cornmeal in a bowl and mix well. Add the melted bacon drippings and mix well. Pour evenly into the hot skillet. Bake at 450 degrees for 15 to 20 minutes or until golden brown. Cut into wedges and butter while hot. Serves 8 to 10.

SALLIE C. DUNPHY, PH.D.

APPETIZERS, BREADS & BEVERAGES

BEVERLY'S SWEET ROLLS

1 cup packed brown sugar
2 to 3 tablespoons ground cinnamon
1/2 cup (1 stick) butter or margarine, melted
2 (10-count) cans refrigerator flaky biscuits
1/2 cup orange marmalade
1/2 to 1 cup finely chopped pecans

Mix the brown sugar and cinnamon in a pie plate and spread evenly over the bottom of the pie plate. Pour the melted butter into a small bowl. Separate the biscuits. Dip the biscuits into the melted butter and coat in the brown sugar mixture. Stand the biscuits on end in a bundt pan coated with nonstick cooking spray. Spoon the orange marmalade over and around the biscuits. Sprinkle with the pecans. Bake at 350 degrees for 38 minutes. Invert immediately onto a serving plate. Let stand for 10 minutes before serving. Serves 20.

ELLEN SHUFFLEBARGER, *Senior Sustainer*

APPETIZERS, BREADS & BEVERAGES

MY GRANDMOTHER'S YEAST ROLLS

3/4 cup shortening
1 cup hot water
1 cup cold water
1/2 cup sugar
1 teaspoon salt
2 eggs, well beaten
1 envelope dry yeast
6 cups all-purpose flour

Combine the shortening and hot water in a bowl. Stir until the shortening is melted. Stir in the cold water, sugar and salt. Add the eggs and mix well. Add the yeast and mix well. Add the flour and mix well. Let stand for 20 minutes. Chill, covered, until ready to bake or shape into rolls and arrange on a greased baking sheet. Let rise in a warm place until doubled in bulk. Bake at 400 degrees for 15 to 20 minutes. Makes 3 to 4 dozen rolls.

ANDREA LUCAS

ORANGE BUTTER

1/2 cup (1 stick) butter, softened
1 1/2 to 2 cups confectioners' sugar
1/4 cup frozen orange juice concentrate, thawed
Grated orange zest to taste

Beat the butter, confectioners' sugar and orange juice concentrate in a bowl until light and fluffy. Stir in the orange zest. Store in an airtight container in the refrigerator. Serve over warm rolls. Makes about 2 cups.

SUSAN WARD

APPETIZERS, BREADS & BEVERAGES

CRUNCHY BREAD TWISTS

1 egg, beaten
1/4 cup Green Goddess salad dressing
2 cups herb-seasoned stuffing mix, coarsely crushed
1/2 cup (2 ounces) grated Parmesan cheese
1 (8-count) can refrigerator crescent rolls

Combine the egg and salad dressing in a small bowl and mix well. Combine the stuffing mix and cheese in a shallow dish or on waxed paper and mix well. Separate the crescent roll dough into four rectangles on a work surface. Press the seams to seal and flatten slightly with a rolling pin. Cut each rectangle lengthwise into four 1-inch strips. Dip each dough strip into the egg mixture and then coat in the stuffing mixture. Twist each strip several times and arrange the strips 1 inch apart on an ungreased baking sheet. Bake at 375 degrees for 15 minutes or until golden brown. Serve warm. Makes 16 twists.

HEATHER THOMAS

APPETIZERS, BREADS & BEVERAGES

CHARITY LEAGUE PUNCH

4 1/2 cups water
1 cup sugar
1 cup amaretto
1 (6-ounce) can frozen lemonade concentrate, thawed
1 (6-ounce) can frozen orange juice concentrate, thawed
1 (2-liter) bottle lemon-lime soda, chilled

Combine the water and sugar in a saucepan. Simmer over medium heat for 15 minutes, stirring frequently. Remove from the heat and stir in the amaretto, lemonade concentrate and orange juice concentrate. Pour into an ice mold, bundt pan or sealable plastic freezer bags. Cover or seal the bags and freeze until firm. Remove to a punch bowl and let stand at room temperature until slushy. Stir in the soda. Serves 12 to 15.

NOTE: *When doubling or tripling this recipe, freeze in original batch portions so that one 2 liter bottle of lemon-lime soda can be added to each portion. This recipe originated in the 1980s and is served at Charity League functions. It has even traveled with the ladies!*

APPETIZERS, BREADS & BEVERAGES

ORANGE CREAMSICLE SMOOTHIE

1 cup fresh orange juice
1/2 sliced frozen banana
1/2 cup nonfat vanilla frozen yogurt
1/2 cup crushed ice

Process the orange juice, banana, frozen yogurt and ice in a blender until smooth. Pour into two glasses and garnish each with an orange slice. Serves 2.

JESSICA SPOKEGAL, *Senior Sustainer*

WASSAIL BOWL

12 small apples, cored (optional)
12 tablespoons packed brown sugar (optional)
1 quart high-quality ale
1 1/2 cups packed light brown sugar
1 large cinnamon stick
2 quarts high-quality ale
1 (750-milliliter) bottle medium-dry sherry
1 teaspoon nutmeg
1/2 teaspoon ginger
2 lemons, thinly sliced

Arrange the apples in a baking dish and top each with 1 tablespoon of the brown sugar. Bake at 350 degrees for 20 to 30 minutes or until tender. Cover with foil and keep warm. Combine 1 quart ale, 1 1/2 cups brown sugar and the cinnamon stick in a large saucepan. Simmer over low heat until the sugar is dissolved, stirring occasionally. Stir in 2 quarts ale, the sherry, nutmeg, ginger and lemon slices. Simmer until heated through, stirring occasionally. Remove and discard the cinnamon stick. Pour into a large heatproof punch bowl and float the apples on top. Serves 15.

SALLIE C. DUNPHY, PH.D.

SOUPS SALADS & SANDWICHES

SOUPS, SALADS & SANDWICHES

TUSCALOOSA CHILI

1 bell pepper, chopped
1 onion, chopped
1 tablespoon olive oil
1 pound ground beef, cooked and drained
2 (1-ounce) packages chili seasoning mix
1 (28-ounce) can diced tomatoes
1 (28-ounce) can puréed tomatoes
1 (10-ounce) can tomatoes with green chiles
1 (16-ounce) can dark red kidney beans
1 (16-ounce) can light red kidney beans
1 (16-ounce) can black beans
1 (16-ounce) can pinto beans
Chili powder to taste

Sauté the bell pepper and onion in the olive oil in a skillet until tender. Add enough water to cover the vegetables and simmer until very tender. Remove to a large saucepan. Add the ground beef, chili seasoning, diced tomatoes, puréed tomatoes, tomatoes with green chiles, dark red kidney beans, light red kidney beans, black beans and pinto beans and stir to mix well. Stir and sprinkle with chili powder three times. Simmer over low heat for 90 minutes, stirring occasionally. Serves 8 to 10.

JANET HOLCOMB, *Senior Sustainer*

SOUPS, SALADS & SANDWICHES

GAME DAY CHILI

2 pounds ground beef
1 (1-ounce) package hot chili seasoning mix
1 (1-ounce) package medium chili seasoning mix
1 (14-ounce) can diced tomatoes
1 (10-ounce) can tomatoes with green chiles
1 (16-ounce) can kidney beans
1 (16-ounce) can chili beans
1 (16-ounce) can black beans
1 (12-ounce) can beer

Brown the ground beef in a large saucepan, stirring until crumbly; drain. Add the hot chili seasoning, medium chili seasoning, diced tomatoes, tomatoes with green chiles, kidney beans, chili beans, black beans and beer and mix well. Bring to a boil, stirring occasionally. Reduce the heat and simmer until halftime, stirring occasionally. Serve with sour cream and shredded Cheddar cheese. Serves 6 to 8.

ANNE FELLER

SOUPS, SALADS & SANDWICHES

MARINER STEW

2 tablespoons butter
1/4 cup all-purpose flour
2 cups cream
1/2 cup brewed coffee
1/4 teaspoon salt
1/2 teaspoon pepper
1/4 teaspoon granulated sugar
1/4 teaspoon brown sugar
1 cup cooked lobster meat, cut into bite-size pieces
1 cup cooked crab meat, cut into bite-size pieces
1/2 cup cooked scallops, cut into bite-size pieces

Melt the butter in a saucepan over medium-low heat. Stir in the flour gradually. Cook until smooth, stirring constantly. Stir in the cream gradually. Stir in the coffee gradually. Cook over medium-low heat for 10 minutes, stirring constantly. Remove from the heat and add the salt, pepper, granulated sugar and brown sugar. Stir until the sugars are dissolved. Stir in the lobster meat, crab meat and scallops. Cook over medium-low heat for 10 to 12 minutes, stirring occasionally. Serves 4 to 6.

ELIZABETH PATTON

SOUPS, SALADS & SANDWICHES

MEXICAN STEW

1 pound ground beef
1 (11-ounce) can Mexicorn
2 (1-ounce) packages taco seasoning mix
2 (4-ounce) cans diced green chiles
2 (10-ounce) cans tomatoes with green chiles
1 onion, chopped
2 (15-ounce) cans black beans

Brown the ground beef in a skillet, stirring until crumbly; drain. Remove to a slow cooker. Add the corn, taco seasoning, green chiles, tomatoes with green chiles, onion and black beans and mix well. Stir in enough water to achieve the desired consistency. Cook on High for 2 to 3 hours. Serve with shredded cheese, sour cream and tortilla chips. Serves 6.

DONNA MOREMAN

IRISH STEW

1 large sweet onion, chopped
1 (10-ounce) can beef consommé
1 pound fresh mushrooms
1 heaping tablespoon chopped garlic
3 cups water
3 pounds stew beef or lamb cubes
1 pound shredded carrots
3 pounds Yukon Gold potatoes
2 (12-ounce) bottles Irish beer
Steak seasoning

Combine the onion, consommé, mushrooms, garlic and water in a slow cooker and mix well. Cook on Low overnight. Stir in the beef, carrots, potatoes, beer and steak seasoning. Cook, covered, on Low for 8 to 10 hours. Serves 6.

THERESA GESSER

SOUPS, SALADS & SANDWICHES

SPICY VEGETABLE SOUP

1 pound ground beef
1 (20-ounce) package frozen mixed vegetables
1 (15-ounce) can chili
1 (14-ounce) can diced tomatoes
1 (10-ounce) can tomatoes with green chiles
1 (12-ounce) can beer
1 (16-ounce) jar salsa

Brown the ground beef in a large saucepan, stirring until crumbly; drain. Stir in the mixed vegetables, chili, diced tomatoes, tomatoes with green chiles, beer and salsa. Bring to a boil and reduce the heat. Simmer for 45 minutes or until the vegetables are tender, stirring occasionally. Serves 8.

ANNE FELLER

SOUPS, SALADS & SANDWICHES

SHERRY'S BEEF AND BEAN SOUP

3 pounds stew beef, ground beef or cooked chicken
4 to 6 (10-ounce) cans chicken broth
12 to 15 cans assorted beans, rinsed and drained
1 (16-ounce) can whole kernel corn
Chili powder to taste
Thyme to taste
Basil to taste
Garlic powder to taste
Bay leaves to taste

Brown the beef in a large saucepan over medium-high heat. Reduce the heat and simmer, covered, until the juices have cooked down. Stir in one can of the broth. Cook, covered, until the liquid has cooked down. Stir in the beans and corn. Stir in enough of the remaining broth to cover the bean mixture. Stir in chili powder, thyme, basil, garlic powder and bay leaves or preferred seasonings. Bring to a boil and reduce the heat. Simmer for 1 hour or until the meat is tender. Remove and discard the bay leaves. Serve immediately to a crowd or freeze in airtight containers for future meals. Serves 30.

SHERRY SCARBOROUGH, *Director, Volunteer Services,*
Hearing & Speech Center, Children's Hospital, Birmingham, Alabama

SOUPS, SALADS & SANDWICHES

CURLY "Q" CHICKEN NOODLE SOUP

1 chicken
3 to 5 cups water
1 (16-ounce) package baby carrots, sliced
4 to 5 ribs celery, sliced
1/4 teaspoon salt
1/8 teaspoon pepper
2 (10-ounce) cans chicken broth
2 chicken bouillon cubes
3 (3-ounce) packages chicken-flavored ramen noodles

Remove the giblets from the chicken and discard. Rinse the chicken inside and out under cold water. Place the chicken in a large saucepan and add 3 to 5 cups water. Cook over medium-high heat for 45 minutes until the chicken is cooked through. Remove the chicken carefully with slotted spoons to a colander and rinse under cold water. Remove the skin and debone the chicken. Tear or shred the chicken into bite-size pieces and return to the saucepan. Stir in the carrots, celery, salt, pepper, broth, bouillon cubes and seasoning packets from the ramen noodles. Reduce the heat to low. Simmer, covered, for 15 minutes. Add one to two packages of the ramen noodles, left whole or broken. Discard the remaining noodles. Cook over medium heat for 3 minutes, stirring occasionally. Serve with grilled cheese sandwiches or goldfish crackers or freeze and save to serve on a cold rainy day. Serves 8.

ANGIE SIMMONS

SOUPS, SALADS & SANDWICHES

POTATO SOUP

1 (16-ounce) package frozen hash brown potatoes
1 small onion, chopped
1/2 rib celery, finely chopped
1 (10-ounce) can condensed chicken broth
3 cups water
1 (10-ounce) can condensed cream of celery soup
2 cups milk
Salt and pepper to taste

Combine the potatoes, onion, celery, broth and water in a saucepan and mix well. Bring to a boil over medium heat, stirring occasionally. Reduce the heat and simmer for 30 minutes. Stir in the soup, milk, salt and pepper. Simmer over low heat for 10 minutes longer. Serves 6 to 8.

KRIS REDDEN

STEAK SALAD

2 pounds sirloin, ribeye or tenderloin steak
1 (8-ounce) package mushrooms, sliced
1/2 cup chopped green onions
1 bunch broccoli, chopped
1 cup sliced celery
1 cup thinly sliced carrots
2 cups grape tomatoes or cherry tomatoes, cut into halves
1 teaspoon chopped fresh dill weed
1 (8-ounce) bottle Italian vinaigrette salad dressing

Grill or broil the steak to medium-rare. Remove to a cutting board and let stand for 1 hour or until cool. Slice into bite-size strips. Combine the steak, mushrooms, green onions, broccoli, celery, carrots, tomatoes and dill weed in a large bowl. Toss to mix. Add the salad dressing and toss to coat. Chill, covered, for 3 hours. Serves 12.

KATHERINE MANUSH

SOUPS, SALADS & SANDWICHES

WILD RICE CHICKEN SALAD

1 (6-ounce) package wild rice
4 chicken breasts, cooked and chopped
1 red bell pepper, diced
2 green onions, chopped
2 garlic cloves, minced
1 tablespoon Dijon mustard
1/2 teaspoon salt
1/4 teaspoon pepper
1/4 teaspoon sugar
1/3 cup seasoned rice wine vinegar
2 avocados
Lemon juice
1 cup chopped pecans, toasted
Lettuce leaves

Prepare the wild rice according to the package directions. Combine the wild rice, chicken, bell pepper and green onions in a bowl and mix well. Whisk the garlic, Dijon mustard, salt, pepper, sugar and vinegar in a small bowl. Add to the chicken mixture and toss to coat. Chill, covered, for 2 to 3 hours. Cut the avocados into small pieces and sprinkle with lemon juice. Add the avocados and pecans to the chicken mixture and toss gently. Spoon onto lettuce-lined salad plates. Serves 6 to 8.

LYNN LLOYD, *President 1993–1994*

TUNA RICE SALAD

1 (6-ounce) package long grain and wild rice
1 (12-ounce) can tuna, drained
1 cup chopped celery
2 tablespoons finely chopped onion
1/2 cup mayonnaise
1/2 cup sour cream
3/4 cup chopped pecans
Salt and pepper to taste

Prepare the rice according to the package directions. Remove to a bowl and let cool. Add the tuna, celery, onion, mayonnaise, sour cream, pecans, salt and pepper and mix well. Chill, covered, for 2 hours or longer. Serve with crackers. Serves 4 to 6.

LISA MCCORMICK, *Senior Sustainer*

VERMICELLI PASTA SALAD

1/3 cup vegetable oil
1/3 cup lemon juice
4 1/2 teaspoons MSG
2 tablespoons seasoned salt
1 (16-ounce) package vermicelli,
  cooked al dente and drained
1 1/4 cups chopped celery
3/4 cup chopped green bell pepper
3/4 cup chopped white onion
1 (10-ounce) jar sliced black olives, drained
1 cup mayonnaise

Whisk the oil, lemon juice, MSG and seasoned salt in a large bowl. Add the pasta and stir to coat. Chill, covered, for 2 days. Add the celery, bell pepper, onion, olives and mayonnaise and mix well. Chill, covered, until ready to serve. Serves 6 to 8.

AMY SCHROEDER, *Senior Sustainer*

SOUPS, SALADS & SANDWICHES

GREAT PASTA SALAD

1 1/2 cups vegetable oil
1 1/2 cups vinegar
1 1/2 cups sugar
1 tablespoon MSG
1 tablespoon dried onion flakes
1 tablespoon chopped fresh parsley
1 teaspoon salt
1 1/2 teaspoons pepper
1 teaspoon garlic powder
Sliced cucumbers
Chopped red onion
Sliced celery
Black or green olives
Sliced carrots
Baby corn
Quartered canned artichoke hearts
Chopped broccoli
16 ounces pasta, cooked al dente and drained

Whisk the oil, vinegar, sugar, MSG, onion flakes, parsley, salt, pepper and garlic powder in a large bowl. Add the cucumbers, onion, celery, olives, carrots, baby corn, artichokes and broccoli or any combination of your favorite vegetables and the pasta and mix well. Chill, covered, until ready to serve. Serves 10 to 12.

LUCY FARMER

SOUPS, SALADS & SANDWICHES

MAMAW'S HOT BACON SALAD

Bibb or leaf lettuce
2 to 4 green onions, chopped
4 slices bacon
2 tablespoons white vinegar
1 teaspoon sugar
Salt and pepper to taste

Fill a bowl with lettuce. Add the green onions and toss to mix. Cook the bacon in a cast-iron skillet until crisp. Remove with a slotted spoon to paper towels to drain; crumble. Remove all but 1/4 cup of the bacon drippings from the skillet. Whisk the vinegar, sugar, salt and pepper into the skillet. Cook just to boiling, whisking occasionally. Pour over the lettuce and green onions and toss lightly to coat. Sprinkle with the crumbled bacon. Serves 4.

LISA MCCORMICK

SOUPS, SALADS & SANDWICHES

MEXICAN SALAD

1 head iceberg lettuce, torn into bite-size pieces
1 bell pepper, sliced
1 small onion, sliced or chopped
1 (15-ounce) can ranch-style beans, drained
2 tomatoes, chopped
1 cup (4 ounces) shredded sharp Cheddar cheese
1 (4-ounce) package corn chips, crushed
1 (8-ounce) bottle Catalina salad dressing

Combine the lettuce, bell pepper and onion in a bowl and toss to mix. Chill, covered, until cold. Add the beans, tomatoes, cheese, corn chips and salad dressing and toss to mix. Serve immediately. Serves 4 to 6.

GWEN VINZANT, *Senior Sustainer*

BROCCOLI CAULIFLOWER SALAD

2 cups broccoli florets
2 cups cauliflower florets
1/2 purple onion, sliced
1 (8-ounce) can sliced water chestnuts, drained
8 ounces bacon, crisp-cooked and crumbled
1/4 cup (1 ounce) grated Parmesan cheese
1 teaspoon basil
1/2 teaspoon salt
1 cup mayonnaise
2 to 4 tablespoons honey
1 (10-ounce) package romaine, torn

Combine the broccoli, cauliflower, onion, water chestnuts, bacon, cheese, basil and salt in a large bowl and toss to mix. Chill, covered, until cold. Combine the mayonnaise and honey in a small bowl and mix well. Pour over the broccoli mixture. Add the romaine and toss to mix. Serves 8.

MARIANNE BRANDON, *President 1997–1998*

SOUPS, SALADS & SANDWICHES

DILL GREEN BEAN SALAD

1/4 cup finely chopped onion
2 to 3 tablespoons dill weed
3 to 4 tablespoons apple cider vinegar
1 cup mayonnaise
2 tablespoons onion salt
4 (14-ounce) cans cut green beans, drained and rinsed

Combine the onion, dill weed, vinegar, mayonnaise and onion salt in a bowl and mix well. Add the green beans and mix gently. Chill, covered, for 8 hours or up to 4 days. Serves 10.

TYRA JOHNSON-PIRTLE

BROCCOLI SLAW

2 (3-ounce) packages chicken-flavored ramen noodles
1 package broccoli slaw
1/2 cup slivered almonds
1 cup sunflower seeds
1/2 cup sugar
1/2 cup olive oil
1/2 cup balsamic vinegar

Remove the seasoning packets from the noodles. Discard one block of noodles. Crumble the remaining block of noodles into a large bowl. Add the broccoli slaw, almonds and sunflower seeds and mix well. Chill, covered, until cold. Whisk the seasoning packets from the ramen noodles, sugar, olive oil and vinegar in bowl. Pour over the broccoli slaw mixture and toss well to coat. Chill, covered, for 20 minutes before serving. Serves 6.

ANDREA LUCAS

ORIENTAL SLAW

1 (3-ounce) package ramen noodles
1 package broccoli slaw
4 green onions, chopped
1 (2-ounce) package slivered almonds, toasted
1/2 cup vegetable oil
1/4 cup apple cider vinegar
1/4 cup sugar
1/2 teaspoon salt
1/4 teaspoon pepper

Remove and discard the seasoning packet from the noodles. Crumble the noodles into a large bowl. Add the broccoli slaw, green onions and almonds and mix well. Whisk the oil, vinegar, sugar, salt and pepper in a bowl. Pour over the broccoli slaw mixture and toss well to coat. Serves 6.

SUSAN WARD

SOUPS, SALADS & SANDWICHES

APPLE AND BLUE CHEESE SALAD

2 tablespoons sherry vinegar
1 tablespoon fresh lemon juice
1 tablespoon honey
1/2 teaspoon salt
1/4 teaspoon pepper
1/3 cup extra-virgin olive oil
10 cups mixed salad greens
4 ounces blue cheese, crumbled
3 large red apples, cored and cut into bite-size pieces
1/2 cup toasted walnuts
1/2 red onion, thinly sliced

Whisk the vinegar, lemon juice, honey, salt and pepper in a bowl. Whisk in the olive oil gradually and whisk until thick. Combine the salad greens, cheese, apples, walnuts and onion in a bowl and toss well. Drizzle the olive oil mixture over the top and toss to coat. Serve immediately. Serves 6 to 8.

NOTE: *You may use Gorgonzola, feta or goat cheese instead of the blue cheese.*

KELLEY EVERS

SOUPS, SALADS & SANDWICHES

CRANBERRY SALAD

1 cup sugar
2 cups fresh cranberries
1 cup water
1 (6-ounce) package strawberry gelatin
1 cup boiling water
1 cup cold water
2 tablespoons lemon juice
1 tablespoon brandy (optional)
3 ounces cream cheese, softened and cut into cubes
1 cup chopped celery
1 cup chopped apple
1/2 cup chopped nuts

Combine the sugar, cranberries and 1 cup water in a saucepan. Bring just to boiling, stirring occasionally. Remove from the heat and cover. Let stand for 5 minutes. Combine the gelatin and 1 cup boiling water in a large bowl. Stir until the gelatin is dissolved. Stir in 1 cup cold water. Stir in the cranberry mixture and lemon juice. Chill until partially set. Fold in the brandy, cream cheese, celery, apple and nuts. Chill, covered, until set. Serves 10 to12.

JOJO STAMEY, *President-Elect 2006–2007*

SOUPS, SALADS & SANDWICHES

AWESOME GRAPE SALAD

8 ounces cream cheese, softened
1 cup sour cream
1 cup granulated sugar
1 teaspoon vanilla extract
2 pounds seedless green grapes, stemmed, washed and dried
2 pounds seedless red grapes, stemmed, washed and dried
1/2 cup packed brown sugar
1 cup chopped pecans

Beat the cream cheese, sour cream, granulated sugar and vanilla in a large bowl until smooth. Fold in the green grapes and red grapes. Spoon into a 9×13-inch baking dish or large serving bowl. Sprinkle with the brown sugar and top with the pecans. Chill, covered, until cold. Serves 10 to 12.

BECKY HARBIN

GREEN GRAPE SALAD

1 cup sour cream
2 to 3 tablespoons packed brown sugar
2 pounds seedless green grapes, stemmed, washed and dried
Chopped pecans (optional)
Raisins (optional)

Combine the sour cream and brown sugar in a bowl and mix well. Add the grapes and toss to coat. Chill, covered, until ready to serve. Sprinkle with pecans and raisins and serve on lettuce-lined salad plates. Serves 4 to 6.

MARTHA PITTS, *Senior Sustainer*

SOUPS, SALADS & SANDWICHES

FROZEN SOUR CREAM FRUIT SALAD

2 cups sour cream
3/4 cup sugar
Dash of salt
2 tablespoons lemon juice
4 slices pineapple, chopped
6 pitted cherries, chopped
1 banana, chopped
1/3 cup chopped pecans

Combine the sour cream, sugar and salt in a bowl and mix well. Stir in the lemon juice. Fold in the pineapple, cherries, banana and pecans. Fill paper-lined muffin cups 3/4 full. Freeze until firm. Remove the paper from the frozen salads and place on lettuce-lined salad plates. Serves 12 to 15.

ELIZABETH PATTON

SOUPS, SALADS & SANDWICHES

FROZEN FRUIT SALAD

8 ounces cream cheese, softened
3/4 cup sugar
12 ounces whipped topping
3 bananas, sliced
2 (10-ounce) packages frozen strawberries, thawed
1 (15-ounce) can crushed pineapple, drained

Beat the cream cheese and sugar in a bowl until smooth. Stir in the whipped topping. Fold in the bananas, strawberries and pineapple. Spoon into one 9×13-inch baking pan or two 8×8-inch baking pans. Freeze, covered, until firm. Serves 15.

MARY CARMAN, *Senior Sustainer*

SOUPS, SALADS & SANDWICHES

HAM DELIGHTS

1 cup (2 sticks) butter or margarine, softened
3 tablespoons mustard
3 tablespoons poppy seeds
1 onion, grated
1 tablespoon Worcestershire sauce
40 small party rolls, split
1 pound boiled or baked ham, shredded
5 to 6 ounces sliced Swiss cheese, cut into 40 squares

Combine the butter, mustard, poppy seeds, onion and Worcestershire sauce in a bowl and mix well. Spread equal portions of the butter mixture over the split sides of the rolls. Spread equal portions of the ham on the bottom half of each roll. Top each with a square of cheese and cover with the top of the rolls. Wrap in foil and arrange on a baking sheet. Bake at 400 degrees for 10 minutes. Serve warm. Makes 40 small rolls.

NOTE: *This recipe is easily doubled.*

SALLIE C. DUNPHY, PH.D.

SOUPS, SALADS & SANDWICHES

CUCUMBER SANDWICHES

8 ounces cream cheese, softened
1 envelope Italian salad dressing mix
3 dashes of Worcestershire sauce
3 dashes of Tabasco sauce
2 teaspoons mayonnaise
1 (16-ounce) loaf sliced cocktail bread
2 cucumbers, peeled and thinly sliced
Dill weed

Combine the cream cheese, salad dressing mix, Worcestershire sauce, Tabasco sauce and mayonnaise in a bowl and mix well. Spread equal portions of the cream cheese mixture over the bread slices. Top each with a cucumber slice and sprinkle with dill weed. Makes 3 dozen sandwiches.

PATTI JENSEN, *Senior Sustainer*

SOUPS, SALADS & SANDWICHES

HOMEMADE PIMENTO CHEESE

8 ounces sharp Cheddar cheese, shredded
8 ounces mild Cheddar cheese, shredded
2/3 cup sliced pimento-stuffed green olives
2 tablespoons olive liquid
3 tablespoons mayonnaise
2 teaspoons Worcestershire sauce
2/3 cup chopped walnuts

Combine the sharp Cheddar cheese and mild Cheddar cheese in a bowl and mix well. Fold in the olives, olive liquid, mayonnaise, Worcestershire sauce and walnuts. Chill, covered, until ready to serve. Serve with crackers, toast points or use as a sandwich filling. Makes about 5 1/2 cups.

ALEXANDRA ALLYN

VEGETABLES & SIDE DISHES

HOLIDAY ASPARAGUS

8 ounces mushrooms
2 tablespoons butter or margarine
3 (12- to 14-ounce) cans asparagus, drained
3/4 cup toasted slivered blanched almonds
1/4 cup finely chopped onion
2 tablespoons butter or margarine
2 tablespoons all-purpose flour
2 cups hot milk
16 ounces shredded Cheddar cheese or Swiss cheese
1/2 teaspoon dry mustard
1/4 teaspoon salt
1/4 cup toasted slivered blanched almonds
Croutons or bread crumbs (optional)

Sauté the mushrooms in 2 tablespoons butter in a skillet until tender. Alternate layers of the asparagus, 3/4 cup almonds and the sautéed mushrooms in a deep baking dish, making two layers. Sauté the onion in 2 tablespoons butter in a saucepan until tender. Stir in the flour. Cook for 3 minutes, stirring constantly. Add the milk and whisk until smooth and thick. Add the cheese and cook until the cheese is melted, stirring constantly. Stir in the dry mustard and salt. Pour evenly over the vegetables in the baking dish. Sprinkle with 1/4 cup almonds and croutons. Bake at 300 degrees for 50 minutes to 1 hour. Serve very hot. Serves 8 to 10.

JAMIE THACKER

VEGETABLES & SIDE DISHES

MARINATED ASPARAGUS

2 pounds asparagus spears, tough ends trimmed
3/4 cup olive oil
1 tablespoon sugar
1/2 cup white balsamic vinegar
4 garlic cloves, minced
1 teaspoon red pepper flakes

Cook the asparagus in a skillet of boiling water for 3 minutes or until tender-crisp; drain. Arrange the asparagus in a 9×13-inch baking dish. Whisk the olive oil, sugar, vinegar, garlic and red pepper flakes in a bowl. Pour evenly over the asparagus. Chill, covered, for 8 hours. Drain before serving. Serves 6.

CAROL ANN MORRISON, *President 2001–2002*

VEGETABLES & SIDE DISHES

BAKED STUFFED AVOCADOS

2 large avocados, pitted and sliced lengthwise
1/8 teaspoon salt
3 tablespoons lemon juice
1/4 cup (1/2 stick) butter
6 tablespoons all-purpose flour
1/4 teaspoon (heaping) salt
1/4 teaspoon freshly ground pepper
1 cup milk
1/2 cup strong brewed coffee
1/4 cup finely chopped pimento
1/4 cup finely chopped onion
1 cup chopped cooked shrimp
2/3 cup grated asiago cheese

Place the avocado halves in a bowl. Mix 1/8 teaspoon salt and the lemon juice in a small bowl. Sprinkle over the avocados. Melt the butter in a saucepan. Stir in the flour. Cook until smooth, stirring constantly. Stir in 1/4 teaspoon salt, the pepper, milk and coffee. Cook until thickened, stirring constantly. Add the pimento, onion and shrimp and mix well. Remove from the heat and let stand for 10 minutes. Spoon the shrimp mixture into the avocado halves and arrange in a baking dish. Sprinkle with the cheese. Add 1/3 inch of water to the bottom of the baking dish. Bake at 350 degrees for 15 minutes. Serve immediately. Serves 6.

ASHLEY HIBBARD

VEGETABLES & SIDE DISHES

BAKED BEANS

1/2 cup chopped onions
1 (1-pound) package smoked sausages, sliced or chopped
1 (16-ounce) can butter beans or lima beans, drained
1 (16-ounce) can kidney beans, drained
1 (16-ounce) can pork and beans, partially drained
3/4 cup packed brown sugar
1/2 cup ketchup
1 teaspoon salt
1 teaspoon pepper
1 teaspoon dry mustard

Sauté the onions in a nonstick skillet until tender. Remove to a large bowl. Add the sausages, butter beans, kidney beans, pork and beans, brown sugar, ketchup, salt, pepper and dry mustard and mix well. Spoon into a baking dish. Bake at 350 degrees for 40 minutes. Serves 6.

LUCY FARMER

LAYERED BROCCOLI CASSEROLE

2 (10-ounce) packages frozen chopped broccoli, cooked and drained
1 onion, finely chopped
1 (10-ounce) can condensed cream of mushroom soup
1 1/2 cups (6 ounces) shredded Cheddar cheese
1 cup mayonnaise
2 eggs, lightly beaten
1 (6-ounce) package stuffing mix

Spread the broccoli over the bottom of a buttered casserole dish. Combine the onion, soup, cheese, mayonnaise and eggs in a bowl and mix well. Pour evenly over the broccoli. Sprinkle with the stuffing mix. Bake at 350 degrees for 30 to 45 minutes. Serves 6 to 8.

MARTHA PITTS, *Senior Sustainer*

VEGETABLES & SIDE DISHES

ROASTED CAULIFLOWER

1 (2 pound) head cauliflower, cut into florets
1 large red bell pepper, cut into 1-inch strips
Garlic-flavored nonstick cooking spray
1/2 teaspoon salt
1/4 teaspoon pepper

Combine the cauliflower and bell pepper in a bowl and toss well. Spread into a greased shallow roasting pan. Spray the vegetables with the cooking spray. Sprinkle with the salt and pepper. Bake at 450 degrees for 20 minutes or until light brown and tender-crisp, stirring twice during roasting. Serves 4 to 6.

KAY HOUSE, *President 1992–1993*

CREAMED CORN

1/2 cup (1 stick) butter, melted
3 tablespoons all-purpose flour
1 cup whipping cream
2 (11-ounce) cans Shoe Peg corn, drained
1/4 teaspoon salt
1/4 teaspoon pepper

Combine the melted butter and flour in a bowl and mix well. Add the cream, corn, salt and pepper. Spoon into a baking dish. Bake at 350 degrees for 30 minutes. Stir before serving. Serves 8.

PATSY TOPAZI, *Senior Sustainer*

VEGETABLES & SIDE DISHES

CORN CASSEROLE

6 tablespoons margarine
3 tablespoons all-purpose flour
2 cups half-and-half
2 (11-ounce) cans Shoe Peg corn, drained

Melt the margarine in a saucepan. Add the flour and stir until smooth. Stir in the half-and-half. Cook over low heat until the mixture is thick, stirring constantly. Stir in the corn. Spoon into a greased baking dish. Bake at 350 degrees for 30 minutes. Serves 8.

KAY GOOLSBY

MAMA'S FRIED CORN

6 to 8 ears fresh corn
3/4 cup water
1/4 cup (1/2 stick) butter
Salt to taste

Stand one ear of corn in a bowl and cut the kernels from the cob with a sharp knife. Scrape the cob to remove any juice. Repeat with the remaining ears of corn. Heat a large skillet over medium-high heat. Add the water, butter, salt and corn with liquid. Cook until tender. Serves 6 to 8.

CHERIE MOODY, *President 2003–2004*

VEGETABLES & SIDE DISHES

CONNOISSEUR'S CASSEROLE

1 (11-ounce) can Shoe Peg corn, drained
1 (16-ounce) can French-style green beans, drained
1/2 cup chopped celery
1/2 cup chopped onion
1 (2-ounce) jar pimentos, drained and chopped
1/2 cup sour cream
1/2 cup (2 ounces) shredded sharp Cheddar cheese
1 (10-ounce) can condensed cream of celery soup
1/2 teaspoon salt
1/2 teaspoon pepper
1 cup butter cracker crumbs
1/4 cup (1/2 stick) butter, melted
1/2 cup slivered almonds

Combine the corn, green beans, celery, onion, pimentos, sour cream, cheese, soup, salt and pepper in a large bowl and mix well. Spoon into a 1 1/2-quart casserole dish. Combine the cracker crumbs, melted butter and almonds in a bowl until crumbly. Sprinkle over the vegetables in the casserole dish. Bake at 350 degrees for 45 minutes. Serves 8 to 10.

NOTE: *This casserole can be frozen.*

DEBBIE MASHBURN, *Senior Sustainer*

VEGETABLES & SIDE DISHES

SWEET GREEN BEANS

3 (14-ounce) cans cut green beans
1/2 cup packed brown sugar
1/2 teaspoon salt
1/2 teaspoon pepper
1/2 teaspoon garlic salt
5 slices bacon, cut into pieces
1/2 cup (1 stick) margarine, cut into pieces

Drain half the liquid from the green beans. Spread the green beans with the remaining liquid over the bottom of a 9×13-inch baking dish. Combine the brown sugar, salt, pepper and garlic salt in a bowl and mix well. Sprinkle over the green beans. Arrange the bacon pieces over the green beans and dot with the margarine. Bake, covered, at 350 degrees for 2 hours. Bake, uncovered, for 1 hour longer. The green beans will be very dark but taste great. Serves 6.

SUZANNE D. BLOCKER, *Supervisor, Speech/Language Pathology Division, Hearing and Speech Department, Children's Hospital, Birmingham, Alabama*

VEGETABLES & SIDE DISHES

GREEN BEAN BAKE

1 (16-ounce) jar Alfredo sauce
2 (9-ounce) packages frozen green beans, thawed
1/4 teaspoon white pepper
1 (2-ounce) can French-fried onions
1 tablespoon grated Parmesan cheese

Combine the Alfredo sauce, green beans, pepper and half the onions in a 1 1/2-quart baking dish and mix well. Sprinkle with the cheese. Bake at 350 degrees for 25 minutes or until hot and bubbly. Sprinkle with the remaining onions and bake for 5 minutes longer. Serves 6.

ANN SONGER

GREEN BEAN AND ARTICHOKE CASSEROLE

3 green onions, chopped
1/3 cup olive oil
1 (15-ounce) can artichoke hearts, drained and chopped
2 (16-ounce) cans French-style green beans, drained
1 tablespoon dried parsley flakes
1 1/2 teaspoons garlic powder
3/4 cup Italian-seasoned bread crumbs
1/2 cup (2 ounces) grated Parmesan cheese

Sauté the green onions in the olive oil in a saucepan. Add the artichokes, green beans, parsley flakes, garlic powder, bread crumbs and cheese and mix well. Spoon into a buttered casserole dish. Bake at 350 degrees for 30 minutes. Serves 6.

MARTHA PITTS, *Senior Sustainer*

VEGETABLES & SIDE DISHES

GARLIC MASHED POTATOES

7 cups cubed, peeled baking potatoes
6 garlic cloves
1/2 cup milk
1/4 cup (1 ounce) grated Parmesan cheese
2 tablespoons margarine
1/2 teaspoon salt
1/8 teaspoon pepper

Cover the potatoes and garlic with water in a saucepan. Bring to a boil and reduce the heat. Simmer for 20 minutes. Drain and remove to a bowl. Add the milk, cheese, margarine, salt and pepper. Beat with an electric mixer at medium speed until smooth. Serves 8.

KAREN TAUNTON

CREAMY CHEESE POTATOES

1 1/4 cups milk
8 ounces cream cheese, softened
1 tablespoon finely chopped chives
1/2 teaspoon dried onion flakes
1/4 teaspoon salt
4 cups cooked cubed peeled potatoes
Paprika to taste

Stir the milk into the cream cheese in a saucepan. Cook over low heat until the mixture is melted and smooth, stirring constantly. Stir in the chives, onion flakes and salt. Add the potatoes and stir gently to coat. Spoon into a 1 1/2-quart baking dish and sprinkle with paprika. Bake at 350 degrees for 30 minutes. Serves 5 to 6.

TERI HIBBARD, *President 2006–2007*

VEGETABLES & SIDE DISHES

HEAVENLY CREAM POTATO CASSEROLE

5 pounds unpeeled red-skinned potatoes
Salt to taste
Pepper to taste
6 ounces cream cheese
1/2 cup (1 stick) butter
1 cup half-and-half
1/2 cup (2 ounce) grated Parmesan cheese
1 teaspoon garlic salt
1 teaspoon dried parsley flakes
1/2 cup (2 ounces) grated Parmesan cheese
Dash of paprika

Cook the potatoes in a saucepan of boiling water until tender; drain. Mash in a bowl and season with salt and pepper. Spoon into a 9×13-inch baking dish. Combine the cream cheese, butter, half-and-half, 1/2 cup cheese, the garlic salt and parsley flakes in the top of a double boiler. Cook over simmering water until melted and hot, stirring frequently. Pour evenly over the potatoes. Sprinkle with 1/2 cup cheese and paprika. Bake at 350 degrees for 30 to 40 minutes or until bubbly. Serves 12.

CORINNE HINDS, *President 2005–2006*

VEGETABLES & SIDE DISHES

HASH BROWN CASSEROLE

1 (32-ounce) package frozen hash brown potatoes
2 (10-ounce) cans condensed cream of potato soup
1 1/2 cups sour cream
1/2 cup (1 stick) margarine, softened
2 cups (8 ounces) shredded sharp Cheddar cheese

Spread the potatoes over the bottom of a greased 9×13-inch baking dish. Combine the soup, sour cream, margarine and cheese in a bowl and mix well. Spread over the potatoes. Bake at 325 degrees for 1 1/2 hours. Serves 12.

JULIE BERTHON

SWEET POTATO CASSEROLE

6 large sweet potatoes
6 tablespoons butter, melted
3/4 cup packed brown sugar
1/2 cup heavy cream
1 teaspoon vanilla extract
1 teaspoon ground cinnamon
1 cup pecan pieces
Miniature marshmallows.

Wrap the potatoes in foil and pierce with a fork. Bake at 325 degrees for 1 hour. Remove to a wire rack to cool. Chill overnight. Remove the foil and cut the potatoes into halves. Scoop out the cooked potatoes into a bowl and discard the skins. Add the melted butter, brown sugar, cream, vanilla and cinnamon. Beat with an electric mixer at medium speed until smooth. Spoon into a greased 2- to 3-quart baking dish. Sprinkle with the pecans. Cover the top with marshmallows. Bake, covered, at 325 degrees for 20 minutes. Bake, uncovered, for 10 minutes longer or until the marshmallows are melted and light brown. Serves 8.

DONNA MOREMAN

VEGETABLES & SIDE DISHES

SQUASH Á LA BAMA

2 pounds summer squash, sliced
1/2 cup (1 stick) margarine, softened
2 eggs, beaten
1 cup mayonnaise
1/4 cup chopped onion
1/4 cup chopped green bell pepper
2 cups (8 ounces) shredded Cheddar cheese
1 (15-ounce) package bread crumbs or cracker crumbs
Chopped pimento to taste

Cook the squash in a saucepan of boiling water until tender; drain. Combine the cooked squash, margarine, eggs, mayonnaise, onion, bell pepper, cheese, bread crumbs and pimento in a bowl and mix well. Spoon into a buttered baking dish. Bake at 350 degrees for 35 to 40 minutes. Serves 12.

TERI HIBBARD, *President 2006–2007*

VEGETABLES & SIDE DISHES

SQUASH CASSEROLE

2 pounds yellow squash, chopped
1 onion, chopped
1 teaspoon salt
2 tablespoons chopped green bell pepper
2 eggs, beaten
1/2 cup milk
1 cup (4 ounces) shredded sharp Cheddar cheese
1/2 cup butter cracker crumbs
2 tablespoons butter, melted
1/2 teaspoon celery seeds
1/2 teaspoon MSG
1/2 teaspoon salt
1/4 teaspoon pepper
1/4 cup butter cracker crumbs
2 tablespoons butter, melted

Combine the squash, onion and 1 teaspoon salt with water to cover in a saucepan. Bring to a boil and reduce the heat. Simmer for 15 minutes or until the vegetables are tender. Drain well and remove to a bowl. Add the bell pepper, eggs, milk, the cheese, 1/2 cup cracker crumbs, 2 tablespoons melted butter, the celery seeds, 1/2 teaspoon salt, the MSG and pepper and mix well. Spoon into a greased baking dish. Sprinkle with 1/4 cup cracker crumbs and drizzle with 2 tablespoons melted butter. Bake at 350 degrees for 35 to 40 minutes or until the center is firm. Serves 6.

CAROL ANN MORRISON, *President 2001–2002*

VEGETABLES & SIDE DISHES

BAKED VEGETABLES

2 yellow squash, sliced
2 zucchini, sliced
3 Roma tomatoes, cut into wedges
2 tablespoons olive oil

1 teaspoon Italian seasoning
Garlic powder to taste
Salt and pepper to taste
Freshly grated Parmesan cheese

Combine the yellow squash, zucchini and tomatoes in a bowl and toss to mix. Add the olive oil, Italian seasoning, garlic powder, salt and pepper and toss to coat. Spread one-third of the vegetables in a baking dish and sprinkle with cheese. Repeat the layers two more times. Bake, covered, with foil, at 350 degrees for 30 to 40 minutes. Serves 4.

DEBBIE SELF

SPINACH-STUFFED SHELLS

2 (9-ounce) packages frozen creamed spinach
12 ounces cream cheese, softened
2 cups (8 ounces) shredded mozzarella cheese

1 (12-ounce) package jumbo pasta shells, cooked al dente and drained
1 (26-ounce) jar spaghetti sauce

Cook the creamed spinach according to the package directions. Remove the spinach to a bowl. Add the cream cheese and mozzarella cheese and mix well. Spoon the spinach mixture into the pasta shells. Spread the spaghetti sauce over the bottom of a baking dish. Top with the pasta shells, stuffed side up. Bake, covered, at 375 degrees for 30 minutes. Bake, uncovered, for 5 to 10 minutes longer. Serves 12.

LYN HENDERSON, *Senior Sustainer*

VEGETABLES & SIDE DISHES

LINGUINI WITH PESTO

2 garlic cloves
1 1/2 cups packed basil leaves
3/4 cup packed flat-leaf parsley
1/2 cup olive oil
1/3 cup pine nuts, toasted
1/4 cup part-skim ricotta cheese

1/2 teaspoon salt
1/4 cup (1 ounce) grated
   Parmesan cheese
12 ounces linguini, cooked
   al dente and drained

Cook the garlic in a saucepan of boiling water for 2 minutes; drain. Process the garlic, basil, parsley, olive oil, pine nuts, ricotta cheese and salt in a food processor until creamy. Remove to a large bowl and stir in the Parmesan cheese. Add the hot pasta and toss to coat. Serve with vegetables or chicken. Serves 6.

MELANIE BONDS, *Senior Sustainer*

MACARONI AND CHEESE

1 cup macaroni, cooked
   al dente and drained
6 ounces shredded Cheddar
   cheese

1 egg, beaten
1/2 cup milk
1 teaspoon salt
1/2 teaspoon pepper

Alternate layers of macaroni and cheese in a 1 1/2-quart baking dish, making two layers. Combine the egg, milk, salt and pepper in a bowl and mix well. Pour evenly over the macaroni and cheese. Bake, covered, at 350 degrees for 25 to 30 minutes. Bake, uncovered, for 5 minutes longer. Serves 3.

KIM MAREK

VEGETABLES & SIDE DISHES

MACARONI AND CHEESE CASSEROLE

2 (10-ounce) cans condensed cream of mushroom soup
1 cup mayonnaise
1/2 cup (1 stick) margarine, softened
1 1/3 cups water
1 small onion, chopped
1 (2-ounce) jar pimentos, drained and chopped
16 ounces Cheddar cheese, shredded
Salt to taste
12 ounces macaroni, cooked al dente and drained

Combine the soup, mayonnaise and margarine in a bowl and mix well. Stir in the water. Add the onion, pimentos, cheese and salt and mix well. Add the macaroni and mix well. Spoon into a casserole dish. Bake at 325 degrees for 30 minutes. Serves 6.

NOTE: *This can be prepared one day ahead. Chill, covered, until ready to bake.*

SUSIE ROWLAND

VEGETABLES & SIDE DISHES

THREE-CHEESE MACARONI

6 tablespoons butter
1/4 cup all-purpose flour
2 cups half-and-half
3 cups (12 ounces) shredded sharp Cheddar cheese
1/3 cup freshly grated Parmesan cheese
3 tablespoons ricotta cheese
1 teaspoon salt
1/2 teaspoon dry mustard
1/4 teaspoon white pepper
16 ounces macaroni, cooked al dente and drained
1/2 cup bread crumbs

Melt the butter in a saucepan. Stir in the flour and cook until smooth, stirring constantly. Stir in the half-and-half gradually. Cook for 10 minutes or until thickened, stirring constantly. Remove from the heat and stir in the Cheddar cheese, Parmesan cheese, ricotta cheese, salt, dry mustard and white pepper. Pour over the macaroni in a large bowl and mix well. Spoon into a 9×13-inch baking dish. Sprinkle with the bread crumbs. Bake, covered, at 325 degrees for 30 minutes. Bake, uncovered, for 5 to 10 minutes longer.
Serves 8 to 10.

VANESSA STRIPLIN

VEGETABLES & SIDE DISHES

GRANDMOTHER'S CORN BREAD DRESSING

5 ribs celery, finely chopped
3 onions, finely chopped
1 bell pepper, finely chopped
1/4 cup (1/2 stick) butter
1 (10-ounce) can condensed cream of chicken soup
4 eggs, beaten
1 teaspoon salt
1 teaspoon celery seeds
5 teaspoons sage
7 cups chicken broth or turkey broth
4 cups crumbled corn bread
4 cups crumbled toasted white bread (about 30 slices)
3 cups diced cooked chicken or turkey (optional)

Sauté the celery, onions and bell pepper in the butter in a skillet until tender. Remove to a large bowl. Add the soup, eggs, salt, celery seeds and sage and mix well. Stir in the broth. Add the corn bread, white bread and chicken and mix well. Spoon into a greased large baking dish. Bake at 350 degrees for 1 1/2 hours. Serves 12.

CHERIE MOODY, *President 2003–2004*

VEGETABLES & SIDE DISHES

GRITS AND GREENS

4 cups chicken broth
4 cups heavy cream
4 cups grits
1 cup (4 ounce) grated Parmesan cheese
1/2 cup (2 ounces) shredded Cheddar cheese
1 cup chopped Roma tomatoes (about 3 tomatoes)
12 ounces frozen collard greens or favorite greens, thawed
1 cup crumbled cooked bacon

Bring the broth and cream to a boil in a large saucepan. Stir in the grits and reduce the heat. Cook until thick and creamy, stirring frequently. Stir in the Parmesan cheese, Cheddar cheese, tomatoes and greens. Cook until heated through, stirring frequently. Sprinkle with the bacon and serve. Serves 16.

NOTE: *Leftovers freeze and reheat well.*

TOOTSIE CHANDLER, *Senior Sustainer*

VEGETABLES & SIDE DISHES

OVEN MUSHROOM RICE

1/4 cup (1/2 stick) butter or margarine
1 cup long grain rice
1 (10-ounce) can condensed chicken broth
1 (10-ounce) can condensed French onion soup
1 (4-ounce) can sliced mushrooms, drained

Melt the butter in a 2-quart baking dish in the oven. Add the rice, broth, soup and mushrooms to the melted butter and mix well. Bake, covered, at 350 degrees for 1 hour. Serves 4.

KELLEY EVERS

VEGETABLES & SIDE DISHES

EASY FRIED RICE

1/4 cup olive oil
4 cups cooked rice
2 garlic cloves, minced
1 (2-ounce) package onion and mushroom soup mix
1/2 cup water
1 tablespoon soy sauce
1 cup frozen peas and carrots, thawed
2 eggs, lightly beaten

Heat the olive oil in a 12-inch skillet over medium heat. Stir in the rice and garlic. Cook for 2 minutes or until the rice is hot, stirring constantly. Dissolve the soup mix in the water and soy sauce in a bowl. Stir into the rice mixture. Cook for 1 minute, stirring constantly. Add the peas and carrots and cook for 2 minutes, stirring constantly. Make a well in the center of the rice mixture and pour in the eggs. Cook until the eggs are set, stirring constantly. Serves 4.

ROBIN RICH

MAIN DISHES

MAIN DISHES

SOUTHERN PORK ROAST

1 (8-pound) Boston butt roast
Salt and pepper to taste
3 large onions, quartered
1 (16-ounce) package baby carrots
12 small red-skinned potatoes

Place the roast, fat side up, in a large baking dish or small roasting pan. Sprinkle all sides of the roast with salt and pepper. Arrange the onions, carrots and potatoes around the roast. Sprinkle the vegetables with salt. Roast at 375 degrees for 4 hours or until the meat is beginning to fall off the bones. Serves 12.

TRACI ALLEN, *Senior Sustainer*

MAIN DISHES

PORK "TENDER" LOIN

1/2 cup teriyaki sauce
2 tablespoons brown sugar
1/4 cup bourbon
4 (12-ounce) pork tenderloins

Combine the teriyaki sauce, brown sugar and bourbon in a shallow dish or sealable plastic bag and mix well. Add the pork and cover or seal the bag. Chill for 8 hours, turning the meat occasionally. Remove the pork to a rack in a roasting pan and discard the marinade. Roast at 400 degrees for 30 minutes or to 160 degrees on a meat thermometer. Remove the meat to a cutting board and thinly slice. Serve with a mustard sauce or other favorite sauce on or with party rolls. Serves 10 to 12.

VANESSA STRIPLIN

MAIN DISHES

FRUIT AND PORK KABOBS

3 pounds cooked boneless pork loin,
   cut into 1-inch cubes
3 apples, cored and cut into wedges
6 apricots, halved
3 green bananas, cut into 1 1/2-inch slices
1 (10-ounce) jar grape jam
2 tablespoons honey
1/4 teaspoon curry powder
1/8 teaspoon ginger

Thread the pork, apples, apricots and bananas alternately onto six skewers. Mix the jam, honey, curry powder and ginger in a saucepan. Cook until the jam is melted, stirring constantly. Grill the kabobs 3 to 5 inches from the heat source until hot, basting often with the jam mixture. Serve with curried rice. Serves 6.

ANN SONGER

MAIN DISHES

STUFFED SHELLS

4 cups ricotta cheese
4 eggs, beaten
16 ounces shredded mozzarella cheese
1 cup (4 ounces) grated Parmesan cheese
1 cup bread crumbs
1 pound bulk pork sausage, cooked and drained
Salt and pepper to taste
1 (12-ounce) package jumbo pasta shells,
    cooked al dente and drained
1 (26-ounce) jar spaghetti sauce

Combine the ricotta cheese and eggs in a bowl and mix well. Add the mozzarella cheese, Parmesan cheese, bread crumbs, sausage, salt and pepper and mix well. Spoon into the pasta shells. Arrange the stuffed shells in a large baking dish, stuffed side up. Pour the spaghetti sauce over the shells. Bake at 350 degrees for 25 minutes or until bubbly. Serves 12.

JILL BISHOP, *Senior Sustainer*

MAIN DISHES

BREAKFAST CASSEROLE

2 cups all-purpose flour
1 cup milk
1 egg, beaten
1 pound bulk pork sausage, cooked and drained
1 1/2 onions, chopped
1 1/2 cups sour cream
1 egg, beaten
1 tablespoon caraway seeds
Dash of paprika

Combine the flour, milk and 1 egg in a bowl and mix well. Spread over the bottom of a nonstick 9×13-inch baking pan. Brown the sausage in a skillet with the onions, stirring until the sausage is crumbly; drain. Sprinkle the sausage and onion over the dough in the baking pan. Combine the sour cream and 1 egg in a bowl and mix well. Spread over the sausage and onions. Sprinkle with the caraway seeds and paprika. Bake at 350 degrees for 20 minutes. Serves 12.

LASLIE MOONEY, *Senior Sustainer*

MAIN DISHES

BEEF BRISKET

1 (4- to 6-pound) beef brisket
Sliced onions
Sliced celery
1 (8-ounce) bottle Italian salad dressing
1 (4-ounce) bottle liquid smoke

Cover the brisket, onions and celery with water in a Dutch oven. Bring to a boil and reduce the heat. Simmer for 2 to 3 hours; drain. Combine the salad dressing and liquid smoke in a bowl and mix well. Pour over the brisket. Chill, covered, overnight. Bake, covered, at 300 degrees for 2 to 3 hours. Serve with cabbage or roasted potatoes and carrots. Serves 6 to 8.

MELANIE BONDS, *Senior Sustainer*

BEEF TIPS WITH RICE

2 pounds beef tips
1 (10-ounce) can condensed French onion soup
1 (10-ounce) can condensed cream of mushroom soup
2 cups hot cooked rice

Combine the beef tips, onion soup and mushroom soup in a slow cooker and mix well. Cook on Low for 8 to 10 hours or until the beef is tender. Serve over the rice. Serves 6.

CHERIE MOODY, *President 2003–2004*

MAIN DISHES

HAMBURGER CORN CASSEROLE

1 1/4 pounds ground beef
3/4 cup chopped onion
1 (16-ounce) can corn, drained
1 (10-ounce) can condensed cream of chicken soup
1 (10-ounce) can condensed cream of mushroom soup
1 cup sour cream
1 (2-ounce) jar diced pimentos, drained
1/2 teaspoon salt
1/4 teaspoon pepper
1/2 teaspoon MSG
3 cups cooked noodles
1 cup bread crumbs
1/4 cup (1/2 stick) butter, melted

Brown the ground beef in a saucepan with the onion, stirring until the ground beef is crumbly; drain. Add the corn, chicken soup, mushroom soup, sour cream, pimentos, salt, pepper and MSG and mix well. Add the noodles and mix well. Spoon into a baking dish. Sprinkle with the bread crumbs and drizzle with the melted butter. Bake at 350 degrees for 45 minutes. Serves 6.

LYN HENDERSON, *Senior Sustainer*

MAIN DISHES

FAKE LASAGNA

1 1/2 pounds ground beef
1 teaspoon salt
1 teaspoon sugar
1 teaspoon Italian seasoning
2 (8-ounce) cans tomato sauce
1 (6-ounce) can tomato paste
5 to 8 ounces medium egg noodles, cooked al dente and drained
2 to 3 cups (8 to 12 ounces) shredded mozzarella cheese
1 cup cream-style cottage cheese
1 cup sour cream

Brown the ground beef in a saucepan, stirring until crumbly; drain. Stir in the salt, sugar, Italian seasoning, tomato sauce and tomato paste. Simmer, covered, over low heat for 20 minutes. Spread the noodles over the bottom of an 8 1/2×11-inch baking dish. Sprinkle half the mozzarella cheese over the noodles. Combine the cottage cheese and sour cream in a bowl and mix well. Spread over the mozzarella cheese in the baking dish. Top with the meat sauce and sprinkle with the remaining mozzarella cheese. Bake at 350 degrees for 20 to 30 minutes. Serves 8.

SUZANNE D. BLOCKER, *Supervisor, Speech/Language Pathology Division, Hearing and Speech Department, Children's Hospital, Birmingham, Alabama*

MAIN DISHES

LASAGNA

1 pound bulk pork sausage, Italian sausage or ground beef
1 garlic clove, minced
1 tablespoon basil
1 1/2 teaspoons salt
1 (16-ounce) can tomatoes
2 (6-ounce) cans tomato paste
3 cups ricotta cheese
2 eggs, beaten
2 teaspoons salt
1/2 teaspoon pepper
3 tablespoons chopped fresh parsley
1/2 cup (2 ounces) grated Parmesan cheese
10 ounces lasagna noodles, cooked al dente, rinsed in cold water and drained
16 ounces mozzarella cheese, thinly sliced

Brown the sausage in a saucepan, stirring until crumbly; drain. Add the garlic, basil, 1 1/2 teaspoons salt, the tomatoes and tomato paste and mix well. Simmer for 45 minutes to 1 hour or until thick, stirring occasionally. Combine the ricotta cheese, eggs, 2 teaspoons salt, the pepper, parsley and Parmesan cheese in a bowl and mix well. Arrange half the noodles in the bottom of a 9×13-inch baking dish. Spread with half the ricotta cheese mixture. Arrange half the mozzarella cheese slices over the ricotta cheese mixture. Spread half the meat sauce over the mozzarella cheese. Repeat the layers. Bake at 375 degrees for 30 minutes. Let stand for 10 to 15 minutes before cutting into squares. Serves 12.

NIKKI HARKINS, *President 2002–2003*

MAIN DISHES

BAKED SPAGHETTI

1 pound ground beef
1 pound bulk hot pork or venison sausage
1 (16-ounce) can diced tomatoes
1 (26-ounce) jar spaghetti sauce
1 cup sliced mushrooms
1 bell pepper, chopped
1 onion, chopped
1/4 cup (1/2 stick) butter
8 ounces cream cheese
16 ounces thin spaghetti, cooked al dente and drained
8 ounces shredded sharp Cheddar cheese
Grated Parmesan cheese

Brown the ground beef and sausage in a saucepan, stirring until crumbly; drain. Stir in the tomatoes and spaghetti sauce. Sauté the mushrooms, bell pepper and onion in the butter in a skillet until tender. Stir into the meat sauce. Add the cream cheese and cook until melted, stirring frequently. Add the spaghetti and mix well. Spoon into a baking dish. Sprinkle with the Cheddar cheese and Parmesan cheese. Bake at 350 degrees for 30 minutes.
Serves 10 to 12.

CORINNE HINDS, *President 2005–2006*

MAIN DISHES

SPAGHETTI CHEESE CASSEROLE

1 1/2 to 2 pounds ground beef
1 (16-ounce) can tomatoes
1 (8-ounce) can tomato sauce
1 (8-ounce) can tomato paste
1/2 cup (1 stick) butter
1/4 cup all-purpose flour
1 teaspoon salt
2 cups milk
1 1/2 cups (6 ounces) shredded sharp
  Cheddar cheese
1/4 cup (1 ounce) grated Parmesan cheese
16 ounces spaghetti, broken in half,
  cooked al dente and drained

Brown the ground beef in a saucepan, stirring until crumbly; drain. Stir in the tomatoes, tomato sauce and tomato paste. Simmer for 30 minutes. Melt the butter in a saucepan. Stir in the flour and salt and cook until smooth, stirring constantly. Stir in the milk gradually. Cook until thickened, stirring constantly. Add the Cheddar cheese and Parmesan cheese and cook until the cheese is melted and the sauce is thickened, stirring constantly. Spread the spaghetti over the bottom of a baking dish. Top evenly with the meat sauce. Pour the cheese sauce evenly over the top. Bake at 350 degrees for 15 to 20 minutes. Serves 8 to 10.

SUSAN STURDIVANT

MAIN DISHES

POPPY SEED CHICKEN

1 chicken, cooked and deboned
1 (10-ounce) can condensed cream of chicken soup
1 cup sour cream
3 tablespoons poppy seeds
1 sleeve (35 crackers) butter crackers, crushed
1/2 cup (1 stick) butter, melted

Spread the chicken in a baking dish. Combine the soup, sour cream and poppy seeds in a bowl and mix well. Pour evenly over the chicken. Sprinkle with the crushed crackers and drizzle with the melted butter. Bake at 350 degrees for 30 minutes. Serves 4.

ROBIN RICH

CHICKEN AND RICE CASSEROLE

1 chicken, cooked and deboned
1 (14-ounce) can chicken broth
1/2 cup rice
1 cup (4 ounces) shredded cheese

Combine the chicken, broth, rice and cheese in a bowl and mix well. Spoon into a baking dish. Bake at 375 degrees for 1 hour. Serves 4.

BEL HART

MAIN DISHES

SAVORY BAKED CHICKEN

1 chicken, or 6 boneless chicken breasts
1/2 cup (1 stick) butter or margarine, melted
2 tablespoons soy sauce
2 tablespoons Worcestershire sauce
2 tablespoon lemon juice
Mushrooms

Place the chicken in a baking dish. Combine the melted butter, soy sauce, Worcestershire sauce and lemon juice in a bowl and mix well. Pour over the chicken. Bake, covered with foil, at 325 degrees for 30 minutes. Bake, uncovered, for 30 minutes. Add the mushrooms and bake for 30 minutes longer or until the chicken is cooked through and the mushrooms are tender. Serves 6.

SABRA RODGERS, *President 2004–2005*

MAIN DISHES

CHICKEN BREAST CASSEROLE

1/2 cup (1 stick) butter or margarine
12 chicken breasts
Salt and pepper to taste
2 (10-ounce) cans condensed cream of mushroom soup
1 cup sour cream
2 1/2 cups slivered almonds

Melt the butter in a greased 9×13-inch baking dish in the oven. Season the chicken with salt and pepper. Arrange the chicken, breast side down, in the melted butter in the baking dish. Bake at 350 degrees for 30 minutes. Turn the chicken over and bake for 30 minutes longer. Turn the chicken over. Combine the soup and sour cream in a bowl and mix well. Spread over the chicken. Bake for 20 minutes. Sprinkle with the almonds. Bake for 10 minutes longer or until the chicken is cooked through. Serves 12.

NOTE: *You may make this with chopped cooked chicken. Eliminate the butter and combine all remaining ingredients in a baking dish and bake at 350 degrees for 30 minutes.*

JOJO STAMEY, *President-Elect, 2006–2007*

MAIN DISHES

CREAMY CHICKEN BAKE

8 boneless skinless
  chicken breasts
8 slices Swiss cheese
1 (10-ounce) can condensed
  cream of chicken soup
1/4 cup dry white wine
1/4 cup (1/2 stick) butter, melted
1 cup herb-seasoned
  stuffing mix

Arrange the chicken in a lightly greased 9×13-inch baking dish. Place one slice of cheese over each chicken breast. Combine the soup and wine in a bowl and mix well. Pour evenly over the cheese. Drizzle the melted butter over the soup mixture and top with the stuffing mix. Bake at 350 degrees for 45 to 50 minutes. Serves 8.

VALLIE PATE, *Senior Sustainer*

GRANDDADDY'S CHICKEN

6 boneless skinless
  chicken breasts
All-purpose flour for dredging
1 to 2 tablespoons butter
1/3 cup teriyaki sauce
1 teaspoon minced garlic
5 1/3 tablespoons butter, melted
1 teaspoon sugar

Dredge the chicken in flour to coat. Melt 1 to 2 tablespoons butter in an electric skillet. Add the chicken and cook until brown on both sides. Remove the chicken to a plate. Combine the teriyaki sauce, garlic, 5 1/3 tablespoons melted butter and the sugar in a bowl and mix well. Add to the skillet. Cook at 315 degrees for a few minutes, scraping any brown bits from the bottom of the skillet. Add the chicken to the skillet. Cook for 2 to 3 minutes per side or until the chicken is hot and cooked through. Serve with hot cooked rice. Serves 6.

TRICIA JOSEPH, *Senior Sustainer*

MAIN DISHES

KING'S RANCH CHICKEN

1 (13-ounce) package nacho cheese-flavored tortilla chips, crushed
6 large chicken breasts, cooked, deboned and cut into bite-size pieces
1 onion, chopped
1 (10-ounce) can condensed cream of mushroom soup
1 green bell pepper, chopped
1 (10-ounce) can condensed cream of chicken soup
16 ounces sliced cheese

Spread the crushed tortilla chips over the bottom of a buttered 9×13-inch baking dish. Top with the chicken and sprinkle with the onion. Spread the mushroom soup over the onion and sprinkle with the bell pepper. Spread the chicken soup over the bell pepper. Arrange the cheese over the top. Bake, covered, at 325 degrees for 20 minutes. Bake, uncovered, for 20 minutes longer. Serves 10.

NOTE: *This can be prepared one day ahead. Chill, covered, until ready to bake.*

CHERIE MOODY, *President 2003–2004*

MAIN DISHES

MEXICAN CHILE CHICKEN

1 onion, chopped
2 tablespoons butter
2 (10-ounce) cans condensed cream of
   chicken soup
1 (12-ounce) can evaporated milk
1 (4-ounce) can diced green chiles
1 (10-ounce) can tomatoes with green chiles
1 package corn tortillas
Butter
4 large chicken breasts, cooked, deboned and
   cut into bite-size pieces
2 cups (8 ounces) shredded sharp
   Cheddar cheese

Sauté the onion in 2 tablespoons butter in a saucepan until tender. Stir in the soup, evaporated milk, green chiles and tomatoes with green chiles. Cook until heated through and blended, stirring constantly. Spread the tortillas with butter and tear into pieces. Spread one-third of the tortillas over the bottom of a greased 9×13-inch baking pan. Top with half the chicken. Pour half the soup mixture evenly over the chicken and sprinkle with half the cheese. Repeat the layers and top with the remaining tortillas. Bake at 350 degrees for 45 to 50 minutes or until bubbly. Serves 8 to 10.

GWEN VINZANT, *Senior Sustainer*

MAIN DISHES

PESTO CHICKEN

3 ounces cream cheese, softened
1/4 cup pesto
1/2 cup finely chopped red bell pepper
6 boneless skinless chicken breasts
1/4 teaspoon salt
1/4 teaspoon pepper
3/4 cup crushed cornflakes or bread crumbs
1/2 teaspoon paprika

Combine the cream cheese, pesto and bell pepper in a bowl and mix well. Flatten the chicken breasts with a mallet to 1/4-inch on a work surface. Sprinkle the chicken with the salt and pepper. Spread 2 tablespoons of the cream cheese mixture over each chicken breast. Roll up and secure with a wooden pick. Mix the crushed cornflakes and paprika in a shallow dish. Coat the chicken rolls in the cornflake mixture and arrange in a 7×11-inch baking dish coated with nonstick cooking spray. Chill, covered, for 8 hours. Bring the chicken to room temperature. Bake, uncovered, at 350 degrees for 35 minutes or until the chicken is cooked through. Let stand for 10 minutes. Remove the chicken rolls to a cutting board and remove the wooden picks. Cut into 1-inch slices. Garnish with basil sprigs. Serves 6.

CHRISTINE MEEHAN

MAIN DISHES

CHICKEN PECAN FETTUCCINI

1 cup pecans, chopped
1/4 cup (1/2 stick) butter or margarine
4 boneless skinless chicken breasts,
  cut into bite-size pieces
1 (8-ounce) package sliced mushrooms
1 cup chopped green onions
1 red bell pepper, thinly sliced
2 garlic cloves, pressed
1/4 cup (1/2 stick) butter
3/4 cup half-and-half
1/2 teaspoon salt
1/2 teaspoon pepper
1 cup freshly grated Parmesan cheese
1/4 cup chopped fresh parsley
8 ounces fettuccini, cooked al dente and drained

Sauté the pecans in 1/4 cup butter in a large skillet for 3 minutes or until the pecans are toasted. Remove with a slotted spoon to a small bowl and keep warm. Add the chicken to the skillet and sauté for 5 to 7 minutes or until the chicken is cooked through. Remove the chicken with a slotted spoon to a large bowl and keep warm. Add the mushrooms, green onions, bell pepper and garlic to the skillet and sauté until the vegetables are tender. Remove the vegetables with a slotted spoon and add to the chicken. Add 1/4 cup butter, half-and-half, salt and pepper to the skillet. Cook for 3 minutes, stirring frequently. Stir in the cheese and parsley. Add to the chicken mixture. Add the hot pasta and toss well. Sprinkle with the pecans and serve immediately. Serves 4.

CAROL ANN MORRISON, *President 2001–2002*

MAIN DISHES

ROTEL CHICKEN SPAGHETTI

4 to 6 chicken breasts
12 ounces spaghetti
1 large onion, chopped
1 large bell pepper, chopped
1/2 cup (1 stick) butter or margarine
1 (10-ounce) can tomatoes with green chiles (Rotel)
1 (15-ounce) can baby peas, drained
16 ounces cheese, shredded or sliced
Salt and pepper to taste

Cook the chicken in a large saucepan of seasoned boiling water until cooked through. Remove the chicken with a slotted spoon to a cutting board. Debone the chicken and cut into chunks. Add the pasta to the boiling broth and cook until al dente. Drain well and remove to a large bowl. Sauté the onion and bell pepper in the butter in a skillet until the vegetables are tender. Add to the pasta. Add the chicken, tomatoes with green chiles, peas, cheese, salt and pepper and mix well. Spoon into one 4-quart baking dish or two 2-quart baking dishes. Bake, covered, at 325 degrees for 1 hour or freeze, covered, to bake at a later time. Serves 8 to 10.

KAREN TAUNTON

MAIN DISHES

PAELLA

3 boneless skinless chicken breasts,
  cut into 1-inch cubes
Salt and pepper to taste
1/2 cup olive oil
1 large yellow onion, chopped
2 garlic cloves, minced
4 tomatoes, peeled, seeded and chopped
5 cups chicken broth
1 (16-ounce) can cannellini beans
8 ounces green beans, trimmed
1/2 teaspoon saffron threads, crushed
1 tablespoon chopped fresh rosemary
2 1/2 cups arborio rice
16 peeled large shrimp
1 tablespoon olive oil
1 cup chicken broth

Season the chicken with salt and pepper. Heat 1/2 cup olive oil in a large skillet over medium heat. Add the chicken and sauté until brown on all sides. Remove the chicken with a slotted spoon to a platter. Add the onion, garlic and tomatoes to the skillet. Cook for 10 minutes, stirring frequently. Stir in the chicken and 5 cups broth and simmer for 10 minutes. Stir in the cannellini beans, green beans, saffron, rosemary and rice. Simmer, without stirring, for 20 minutes or until the liquid is almost absorbed. Season the shrimp with salt and pepper. Heat 1 tablespoon olive oil in a skillet over high heat. Add the shrimp and sauté for 2 minutes or until the shrimp turn pink. Stir in 1 cup broth. Pour the shrimp and broth over the rice mixture in the large skillet. Remove from the heat and cover. Let stand for 10 minutes. Serve with lemon wedges. Serves 6 to 8.

MARY SCOTT PEARSON

MAIN DISHES

CRUNCHY CHICKEN BAKE

3 cups chopped cooked chicken
1/2 cup slivered almonds
1 (8-ounce) can sliced water chestnuts, drained
1 (10-ounce) can condensed cream of mushroom soup
1/4 cup chopped pimento
1 tablespoon chopped fresh parsley
1/4 teaspoon celery salt
1/8 teaspoon pepper
1/8 teaspoon paprika
1/2 cup (2 ounces) shredded sharp Cheddar cheese
Crushed butter crackers or canned French-fried onions (optional)

Combine the chicken, almonds, water chestnuts, soup, pimento, parsley, celery salt, pepper and paprika in a bowl and mix well. Spoon into a 1 1/2-quart baking dish. Sprinkle with the cheese and top with crushed crackers. Bake at 350 degrees for 30 minutes. Serves 6.

SUSIE ROWLAND

MAIN DISHES

CHICKEN DIVAN

2 (10-ounce) packages frozen broccoli spears
2 cups sliced cooked chicken
2 (10-ounce) cans condensed cream of chicken soup
1 cup mayonnaise
1 teaspoon lemon juice
1/2 teaspoon curry powder
1/2 cup (2 ounces) shredded Cheddar cheese
1/2 cup soft bread crumbs

Cook the broccoli in a saucepan of boiling salted water until tender; drain. Arrange the broccoli spears over the bottom of a greased 7×11-inch baking dish. Arrange the sliced chicken over the broccoli. Combine the soup, mayonnaise, lemon juice and curry powder in a bowl and mix well. Spread evenly over the chicken. Sprinkle with the cheese and top with the bread crumbs. Bake at 350 degrees for 25 to 30 minutes or until heated through. Serves 6.

JULIE BERTHON

MAIN DISHES

RED WINE VINEGAR CHICKEN

4 to 6 chicken thighs
Olive oil
2 to 3 garlic cloves, crushed
2 to 3 tablespoons chopped fresh parsley
1 cup red wine vinegar
3/4 cup water

Brown the chicken in a small amount of olive oil in a skillet for 3 to 5 minutes per side. Remove the chicken to a platter. Add additional olive oil to the skillet if needed. Add the garlic and parsley to the skillet and sauté until the garlic is tender. Stir in the vinegar and water. Cook for several minutes or until light brown, scraping any brown bits from the bottom of the skillet. Add the chicken and reduce the heat. Simmer for 1 hour or until the chicken is cooked through, reducing the heat, if necessary. Serves 4 to 6.

NOTE: *You may double all ingredients except the chicken, if desired.*

TRICIA JOSEPH, *Senior Sustainer*

MAIN DISHES

MARINATED QUAIL

1/2 cup white wine vinegar
6 tablespoons red burgundy
1/2 teaspoon celery salt
1/2 teaspoon lemon pepper
1/4 teaspoon onion salt
1/4 teaspoon ground sage
1/4 teaspoon thyme
2 teaspoons bacon drippings or extra-virgin olive oil
6 to 12 quail, rinsed and dried
1 cup (2 sticks) butter, melted
Cooked wild rice

Combine the vinegar, burgundy, celery salt, lemon pepper, onion salt, sage, thyme and bacon drippings in a large baking dish and mix well. Add the quail and turn to coat. Chill, covered, for 24 hours, turning the quail several times during marinating. Bake at 300 degrees for 20 minutes, basting often with the marinade. Remove the quail and discard the marinade. Grill the quail over hot coals for 15 to 20 minutes or until cooked through, basting often with the melted butter. Serve over wild rice. Serves 6 to 8.

TYRA JOHNSON-PIRTLE

MAIN DISHES

MILE MARKER FISH

2 tomatoes, sliced
1/2 onion, thinly sliced
1/2 red bell pepper, cut into strips
1/2 yellow bell pepper, cut into strips
1/2 green bell pepper, cut into strips
3 tablespoons bread crumbs
Salt and pepper to taste
1 1/2 pounds grouper fillets
1/2 cup white wine
1/4 cup (1/2 stick) butter
1 tablespoon lemon juice
3 tablespoons grated Parmesan cheese
Dash of paprika

Arrange the tomatoes over the bottom of a lightly buttered 9×13-inch baking dish. Layer the onion, red bell pepper, yellow bell pepper and green bell pepper over the tomatoes. Sprinkle with the bread crumbs, salt and pepper. Arrange the fish fillets over the top. Combine the wine, butter and lemon juice in a saucepan. Cook until the butter is melted, stirring frequently. Pour evenly over the fish. Sprinkle with the cheese and paprika. Bake at 350 degrees for 30 minutes or until the fish flakes easily. Serves 6.

NOTE: *Red snapper, flounder or tilapia fillets also work well.*

KAY HOUSE, *President 1992-1993*

MAIN DISHES

ROASTED SALMON STEAKS

2 tablespoons Dijon mustard
1 tablespoon chopped fresh dill weed
2 teaspoons honey
2 teaspoons white wine vinegar
1 teaspoon dried celery flakes
1/4 teaspoon freshly ground pepper
4 (4-ounce) salmon steaks

Combine the Dijon mustard, dill weed, honey, vinegar, celery flakes and pepper in a bowl and mix well. Spread equal portions of half the mustard mixture over one side of the salmon steaks. Coat a large ovenproof skillet with nonstick cooking spray. Heat in a 500 degree oven until hot. Arrange the salmon, coated side down, in the hot skillet. Roast at 500 degrees for 5 minutes. Spread equal portions of the remaining mustard mixture over the salmon steaks. Turn the salmon over gently. Roast for 3 minutes longer or to desired doneness. Serves 4.

FAY DINKEN, *Senior Sustainer*

MAIN DISHES

NEWPORT CRAB

5 1/3 tablespoons butter
1 cup chopped celery
1/4 cup chopped onion
1/4 cup chopped green bell pepper
1 (4-ounce) can mushrooms, drained
3 tablespoons butter
2 tablespoons all-purpose flour
1/2 cup milk
1/2 teaspoon salt
Pepper to taste
1 cup mayonnaise
1/2 teaspoon Worcestershire sauce
2 cups crab meat
3 cups cooked rice
Buttered bread crumbs

Heat 5 1/3 tablespoons butter in a skillet. Sauté the celery, onion, bell pepper and mushrooms until tender. Melt 3 tablespoons butter in a saucepan. Stir in the flour. Cook until smooth, stirring constantly. Stir in the milk, salt and pepper. Cook until thickened, stirring constantly. Stir in the mayonnaise; do not let boil. Stir in the Worcestershire sauce and crab meat. Pour evenly over the rice in a baking dish. Top with bread crumbs. Bake at 350 degrees for 30 minutes or until bubbly. Serves 4 to 6.

JAMIE THACKER

MAIN DISHES

SCALLOPS THERMIDOR

1 (4-ounce) can mushrooms
1 pound scallops, cut into halves
4 to 5 scallions, chopped
1/4 cup (1/2 stick) butter
1/4 cup all-purpose flour
1 cup milk
1 teaspoon salt
1/2 teaspoon dry mustard
1/8 teaspoon cayenne pepper
2 tablespoons white wine
Grated Parmesan cheese
Paprika

Drain the mushrooms, reserving the liquid. Sauté the drained mushrooms, scallops and scallions in the butter in a skillet for 5 to 6 minutes. Remove the scallops, mushrooms and scallions with a slotted spoon to a bowl. Add the flour to the skillet and cook until smooth, stirring constantly. Stir in the milk and reserved mushroom liquid gradually. Cook until thickened, stirring constantly. Stir in the salt, dry mustard and cayenne pepper. Add the scallops, mushrooms, scallions and wine and mix well. Spoon into well greased individual shells or ramekins. Sprinkle with cheese and paprika. Bake at 400 degrees for 12 to 15 minutes or until golden brown. Serves 4.

ANN SONGER

MAIN DISHES

SHRIMP CASSEROLE

1 onion, chopped
1 bell pepper, chopped
1 cup mushrooms
2 tablespoons butter
1 1/2 pounds peeled cooked medium to large shrimp
5 to 8 cups cooked rice
1 (10-ounce) can condensed cream of shrimp soup
1 cup milk
1 sleeve (35 crackers) butter crackers, crushed
2 tablespoons butter, melted

Sauté the onion, bell pepper and mushrooms in 2 tablespoons butter in a skillet until the vegetables are tender. Stir in the shrimp and remove from the heat. Spread the rice over the bottom of a casserole dish. Top with the shrimp mixture. Combine the soup and milk in a bowl and mix well. Pour evenly over the shrimp mixture. Combine the crushed crackers and melted butter in a bowl. Sprinkle over the soup mixture. Bake at 350 degrees for 30 to 45 minutes. Serves 6 to 8.

DONNA CONKLIN

MAIN DISHES

EASY SKILLET RAVIOLI

1 (16-ounce) package frozen cheese ravioli
2 1/4 cups water
1/2 teaspoon salt

1 (26-ounce) jar spaghetti sauce
1/4 cup heavy cream, half-and-half or milk

Combine the ravioli, water and salt in a nonstick 12-inch skillet or nonstick 4-quart saucepan. Bring to a boil over high heat. Boil for 5 minutes, stirring frequently. Stir in the spaghetti sauce and reduce the heat to medium. Cook, covered, until thickened, stirring occasionally. Stir in the cream and cook until heated through. Serves 4.

DINA MANLY

PASTA WITH VODKA SAUCE

10 garlic cloves, chopped
1/4 cup olive oil
1/4 cup vodka
1 (28-ounce) can crushed tomatoes
1/2 cup heavy cream
1/2 cup (2 ounces) grated Parmesan cheese

2 tablespoons dried parsley flakes
1 pound fresh deveined peeled shrimp (optional)
Cooked penne

Sauté the garlic in the olive oil in a skillet until tender. Stir in the vodka and tomatoes and reduce the heat. Stir in the cream. Simmer for 10 minutes. Stir in the cheese and parsley flakes. Add the shrimp and cook just until the shrimp turn pink, stirring frequently. Serve over hot pasta. Serves 4.

PATSY TOPAZI, *Senior Sustainer*

MAIN DISHES

BAKED ZITI

8 ounces mozzarella cheese, shredded
2 cups cottage cheese
1 (26-ounce) jar spaghetti sauce
1 teaspoon oregano
Salt and pepper to taste
16 ounces ziti, cooked al dente and drained

Combine the mozzarella cheese, cottage cheese, spaghetti sauce, oregano, salt and pepper in a bowl and mix well. Stir in the pasta. Spoon into a large baking dish. Bake at 350 degrees for 30 to 45 minutes or until bubbly. Serves 8.

LUCY FARMER

BEST EVER QUICHE

4 to 6 ounces Swiss cheese, shredded
1 unbaked (9-inch) pie shell
8 slices bacon, crisp-cooked and crumbled
4 ounces mushrooms
Butter
3 eggs, beaten
1 cup whipping cream
1/4 teaspoon salt
1/4 teaspoon dry mustard

Spread most of the cheese over the bottom of the pie shell. Sprinkle with the bacon. Sauté the mushrooms in a small amount of butter in a skillet until tender. Spoon the mushrooms over the bacon. Combine the eggs, cream, salt and dry mustard in a bowl and mix well. Pour over the mushrooms. Sprinkle the remaining cheese over the top. Bake at 325 degrees for 45 minutes or until set. Remove to a wire rack and let cool for 10 minutes before serving. Serves 6.

MARIANNE BRANDON, *President 1997–1998*

MAIN DISHES

SOUR CREAM QUICHE

4 eggs, lightly beaten
1 cup sour cream
8 ounces shredded Swiss cheese
4 slices bacon, crisp-cooked and crumbled
1/2 cup diced ham
1/4 cup sliced green onions (optional)
1 partially baked (9-inch) pie shell

Combine the eggs and sour cream in a bowl and mix well. Stir in the cheese, bacon, ham and green onions. Pour into the pie shell. Bake at 350 degrees for 30 minutes. Cover loosely with foil and bake for 15 minutes longer or until golden brown. Serves 6.

NIKKI HARKINS, *President 2002–2003*

SOUTHWESTERN EGG CASSEROLE

2 (4-ounce) cans diced green chiles
16 ounces each sharp Cheddar cheese and Monterey Jack cheese, shredded
1 egg yolk
1 tablespoon all-purpose flour
1 teaspoon salt
1/8 teaspoon pepper
3/4 cup evaporated milk
7 egg whites
1 tomato, diced

Mix the first three ingredients in a bowl. Spread over the bottom of a buttered 12×18-inch baking dish. Beat the egg yolk and flour in a large bowl. Stir in the salt, pepper and evaporated milk. Beat the egg whites in a bowl until stiff. Fold the egg whites into the egg yolk mixture. Pour over the cheese mixture. Separate the cheese mixture gently with a fork to allow the egg mixture to flow to the bottom of the baking dish. Bake at 325 degrees for 30 minutes. Sprinkle with the tomato. Bake for 30 minutes longer. Serves 10 to 12.

ANGIE SIMMONS

DESSERTS

DESSERTS

APPLE DUMPLINGS

1 (8-count) can refrigerator crescent rolls
2 large apples, peeled, cored and halved
2 tablespoons butter, melted
1/4 cup sugar
1 1/2 teaspoons ground cinnamon
1/4 cup orange juice

Separate the crescent dough into four rectangles on a work surface. Press the seams to seal. Place one apple half in the center of each dough rectangle. Bring the corners of the dough together and pinch to seal. Arrange in a lightly greased 9×9-inch baking dish. Drizzle with the melted butter. Mix the sugar and cinnamon in a bowl. Sprinkle evenly over the dumplings. Pour the orange juice into the bottom of baking dish. Bake, covered, at 400 degrees for 35 minutes. Serve hot with whipped cream or vanilla ice cream. Serves 4.

ANGIE SIMMONS

DESSERTS

APPLE CRUNCH

5 apples, peeled, cored
 and sliced
1/2 cup granulated sugar
1 cup all-purpose flour
1/2 cup packed brown sugar

1/2 teaspoon ground cinnamon
1/4 teaspoon salt
1/2 cup (1 stick) butter
 or margarine

Spread the apples over the bottom of a lightly buttered baking dish. Sprinkle with the granulated sugar. Combine the flour, brown sugar, cinnamon and salt in a bowl and mix well. Cut in the butter with a pastry blender or fork until crumbly. Sprinkle over the apples. Bake at 325 degrees for 1 hour. Remove to a wire rack to cool. Serves 6 to 8.

ASHLEY HIBBARD

APPLE TURNOVERS

1 (2-crust) refrigerator
 pie pastry
1 egg white, lightly beaten

1 (21-ounce) can apple or
 cherry pie filling
Sugar (optional)

Unfold the pastry on a work surface. Cut each pastry into quarters and brush the edges with egg white. Spread 1/4 cup of pie filling over half of each pastry wedge. Fold the dough over the filling and press with a fork to seal the edges. Arrange on two baking sheets coated with nonstick cooking spray. Brush the turnovers with egg white and sprinkle with sugar. Cut three slits in each turnover. Bake at 375 degrees for 20 to 25 minutes or until golden brown. Remove the turnovers to a wire rack to cool. Serve warm or at room temperature. Serves 8.

DEBBIE THOMPSON, *Senior Sustainer*

DESSERTS

FESTIVE BANANA SPLIT CAKE

2 cups graham cracker crumbs
1/2 cup (1 stick) margarine, melted
1 cup (2 sticks) margarine, softened
2 eggs
1 teaspoon vanilla extract
1 (16-ounce) package confectioners' sugar
1 (8-ounce) can crushed pineapple, drained
4 large bananas, sliced
1 large container whipped topping
Chopped nuts

Combine the graham cracker crumbs and 1/2 cup melted margarine in a bowl and mix until crumbly. Press over the bottom of a 9×13-inch baking pan. Beat 1 cup margarine, the eggs, vanilla and confectioners' sugar in a bowl until light and fluffy. Spread over the graham cracker crust. Spread the pineapple over the confectioners' sugar mixture. Arrange the banana slices over the pineapple. Spread with the whipped topping and sprinkle with nuts. Garnish with maraschino cherries. Serves 15.

NOTE: *If you are concerned about using raw eggs, use eggs pasteurized in their shells, which are sold at some specialty food stores, or use an equivalent amount of pasteurized egg substitute.*

HEATHER THOMAS

DESSERTS

WHITE CHOCOLATE BREAD PUDDING

4 cups heavy cream
1 loaf crusty French bread, torn into small pieces
3 eggs, lightly beaten
2 cups sugar
2 tablespoons vanilla extract
2 cups (12 ounces) white chocolate chips
2 tablespoons baking cocoa
2 cups (12 ounces) white chocolate chips
1 cup heavy cream

Pour 4 cups cream over the bread in a large bowl. Let stand for 30 minutes, stirring occasionally. Add the eggs, sugar and vanilla and mix well. Stir in 2 cups white chocolate chips. Pour into a greased 9×13-inch baking dish. Bake at 350 degrees for 45 to 55 minutes. Sift the baking cocoa evenly over the hot pudding. Combine 2 cups white chocolate chips and 1 cup cream in a microwave-safe bowl. Microwave on High for 2 minutes. Whisk to mix. Microwave on High until melted and smooth, whisking after each minute. Spoon the warm bread pudding into serving bowls and top with the hot white chocolate sauce. Serves 15.

SUSAN JESSUP

DESSERTS

BROWN SUGAR CHEESECAKE

2 cups graham cracker crumbs
6 tablespoons granulated sugar
6 tablespoons butter, melted
48 ounces cream cheese, softened
2 1/2 cups packed brown sugar
1/4 cup all-purpose flour
6 eggs
1 tablespoon vanilla extract

Combine the graham cracker crumbs, granulated sugar and melted butter in a bowl and mix until crumbly. Press over the bottom of two 9-inch springform pans. Bake at 300 degrees for 10 minutes. Remove to a wire rack to cool. Beat the cream cheese, brown sugar and flour in a bowl with an electric mixer at medium speed until light and fluffy. Add the eggs, one at a time, beating well after each addition. Stir in the vanilla. Pour into the prepared pans. Bake at 300 degrees for 45 to 50 minutes. Remove to a wire rack to cool completely. Loosen from the side of the pans with a sharp knife and remove the sides. Serve immediately or freeze, covered, until ready to serve. Thaw before serving. Serves 24.

KATHERINE MANUSH

DESSERTS

CHOCOLATE COOKIE FREEZE

28 chocolate sandwich cookies, finely crushed
1/4 cup (1/2 stick) butter, melted
1/2 gallon vanilla ice cream, softened
1 cup sugar
1 (5-ounce) can evaporated milk
4 ounces semisweet chocolate
6 tablespoons butter
1 teaspoon vanilla extract
12 ounces whipped topping
1 cup chopped nuts

Combine the crushed cookies and 1/4 cup melted butter in a bowl until crumbly. Press over the bottom of a greased 9×13-inch baking pan. Freeze until firm. Spread the ice cream evenly over the cookie layer. Freeze until firm. Combine the evaporated milk, chocolate and 6 tablespoons butter in a saucepan. Bring to a boil and cook for 1 minute, stirring frequently. Remove from the heat and stir in the vanilla. Let cool to room temperature. Spread over the ice cream layer. Spread with the whipped topping and sprinkle with the nuts. Freeze until firm. Garnish with chocolate shavings. Serves 15.

JENNIFER KUSTA

DESSERTS

CHOCOLATE ÉCLAIR CAKE

3 tablespoons baking cocoa
1/4 cup evaporated milk
1/2 cup (1 stick) butter
1 teaspoon vanilla extract
2 (3-ounce) packages French vanilla instant pudding mix
3 cups cold milk
1 large container whipped topping
1 (14-ounce) package graham crackers

Combine the baking cocoa, evaporated milk, butter and vanilla in a saucepan. Bring to a boil, stirring constantly. Remove from the heat and let cool. Chill, covered, until cold. Whisk the pudding mix and cold milk in a bowl for 2 minutes. Fold in the whipped topping. Fit one-third of graham crackers over the bottom of a 9×13-inch baking pan. Spread with half the pudding mixture. Top with one-third of the graham crackers. Spread with the remaining pudding mixture. Top with the remaining graham crackers. Pour the cold chocolate mixture evenly over the top. Chill, covered, overnight. Serves 15.

SANDRA TRAYWICK, *Senior Sustainer*

DESSERTS

CHOCOLATE PEANUT BUTTER ICE CREAM

1 cup evaporated milk
4 ounces unsweetened chocolate
2 eggs
3/4 cup sugar
4 to 6 tablespoons chunky or creamy
   peanut butter
2 1/3 cups evaporated milk

Combine 1 cup evaporated milk and chocolate in a saucepan. Cook over medium heat until melted and smooth, stirring frequently. Combine the eggs and sugar in a large bowl and beat well. Add the peanut butter and beat well. Stir in the hot chocolate mixture. Stir in 2 1/3 cups evaporated milk. Pour into an ice cream freezer container. Freeze using the manufacturer's directions. Makes 2 quarts.

NOTE: *If you are concerned about using raw eggs, use eggs pasteurized in their shells, which are sold at some specialty food stores, or use an equivalent amount of pasteurized egg substitute.*

TONI WOLFE

DESSERTS

CHOCOLATE CHESS PIE

3 cups sugar
6 tablespoons baking cocoa
1/2 cup (1 stick) butter, melted
1 1/3 cups evaporated milk
4 eggs, beaten
2 teaspoons vanilla extract
2 unbaked (9-inch) pie shells

Process the sugar and baking cocoa in a blender for a few seconds. Add the melted butter, evaporated milk, eggs and vanilla and process until smooth. Pour into the pie shells. Bake at 325 degrees for 40 minutes. Remove to a wire rack to cool. Serves 12.

SUSAN WARD

CHOCOLATE CHIP PECAN PIE

4 eggs, lightly beaten
2 cups sugar
1 cup (2 sticks) butter or margarine, softened
2 cups (12 ounces) chocolate chips, melted
2 cups chopped pecans
2 teaspoons vanilla extract
2 unbaked (9-inch) pie shells

Combine the eggs, sugar, butter, melted chocolate chips, pecans and vanilla in a bowl and mix well. Pour into the pie shells. Bake at 350 degrees for 25 to 30 minutes. Remove to a wire rack to cool. Serves 16.

JULIE WOODSON

DESSERTS

CHOCOLATE OUTRAGEOUS PIE

1 cup (2 sticks) unsalted butter, softened
8 ounces cream cheese, softened
2 cups sugar
4 ounces unsweetened chocolate, melted and slightly cooled
1 teaspoon vanilla extract
4 eggs
1 baked (9-inch) pie shell

Beat the butter and cream cheese in a bowl with an electric mixer until light and fluffy. Beat in the sugar gradually. Beat until the sugar is dissolved and the mixture is creamy. Beat in the melted chocolate and vanilla. Add the eggs, one at a time, beating for 5 minutes after each addition. Pour into the pie shell. Chill for 4 hours before serving. Garnish with whipped cream and grated chocolate. Serves 8.

NOTE: *If you are concerned about using raw eggs, use eggs pasteurized in their shells, which are sold at some specialty food stores, or use an equivalent amount of pasteurized egg substitute.*

JULIE WOODSON

NUT FUDGE PIE

3 eggs, lightly beaten
1/2 cup packed brown sugar
1/4 cup all-purpose flour
1/4 cup (1/2 stick) butter, melted
1 teaspoon vanilla extract
2 cups (12 ounces) chocolate chips, melted
1 1/2 cups walnut or pecan pieces
1 unbaked (9-inch) pie shell

Combine the eggs, brown sugar, flour, melted butter and vanilla in a bowl and mix well. Stir in the melted chocolate and nuts. Pour into the pie shell. Bake at 375 degrees for 30 minutes. Remove to a wire rack to cool completely. Serve with vanilla ice cream. Serves 8.

MARY SCOTT PEARSON

LEMON ICEBOX PIE

Juice of 2 lemons
1 (14-ounce) can sweetened condensed milk
1 container whipped topping
1 (9-inch) graham cracker pie shell

Beat the lemon juice, sweetened condensed milk and most of the whipped toping in a bowl until smooth. Spoon into the pie shell. Chill, covered, until cold. Garnish with the remaining whipped topping. Serves 6.

ALEXANDRA ALLYN

DESSERTS

CRUSTED FRESH LEMON BLUEBERRY PIE

PASTRY
2 cups all-purpose flour, sifted
1 teaspoon salt
1/2 teaspoon grated lemon zest
2/3 cup shortening
4 to 6 tablespoons cold water
1 tablespoon lemon juice

FILLING
4 cups fresh blueberries
3/4 to 1 cup sugar
3 tablespoons all-purpose flour
1/2 teaspoon grated lemon zest
Dash of salt
1 to 2 teaspoons lemon juice
1 tablespoon butter or margarine, cut into small pieces

For the pastry, sift the flour and salt into a bowl. Stir in the lemon zest. Cut in the shortening with a pastry blender or fork until the mixture resembles small peas. Mix the cold water and lemon juice in a small bowl. Sprinkle gradually over the flour mixture, tossing gently with a fork to moisten and form a dough. Divide the dough in half and shape each half into a ball. Roll out each ball on a lightly floured work surface to a 1/8-inch-thick circle. Fit one pastry circle into a 9-inch pie plate.

For the filling, combine the blueberries, sugar, flour, lemon zest and salt in a bowl and toss gently to mix. Spoon into the pastry-lined pie plate. Drizzle with the lemon juice and dot with the butter. Top with the other pastry circle and flute the edges to seal. Cut small slits in the top or prick with a fork. Sprinkle with additional sugar, if desired. Bake at 400 degrees for 35 to 40 minutes. Remove to a wire rack to cool. Serves 6.

BECKY CRUM, *President 1991–1992*

DESSERTS

SOUTHERN PECAN PIE

3 eggs, lightly beaten
1/2 cup sugar
1 cup dark corn syrup
1/4 teaspoon salt
2 teaspoons vanilla extract
1/4 cup (1/2 stick) margarine, melted
2 tablespoons all-purpose flour
1 cup pecan pieces
1 unbaked (9-inch) pie shell

Combine the eggs, sugar, corn syrup, salt, vanilla, melted margarine and flour in a bowl and mix well. Spread the pecans over the bottom of the pie shell. Pour the egg mixture into the pie shell. Cover the edge of the pie shell with foil. Bake at 375 degrees for 15 minutes. Reduce the heat to 350 degrees and bake for 20 minutes longer or until the center is firm. Remove to a wire rack to cool. Serves 8.

DENISE LEWIS

OOEY GOOEY CAKE

1 (2-layer) package devil's food cake mix
1 (14-ounce) can sweetened condensed milk
1 (12-ounce) jar caramel ice cream topping
1 container whipped topping

Prepare and bake the cake mix according to the package directions for a 9×13-inch baking pan. Remove to a wire rack and poke holes through to the bottom of the cake with a skewer. Combine the sweetened condensed milk and caramel topping in a bowl and mix well. Pour gradually over the hot cake, allowing the mixture to soak through the cake. Let cool completely. Chill, covered, for 24 to 48 hours. Remove from the refrigerator 20 minutes before serving. Spread with the whipped topping and garnish with shavings of your favorite candy bar. Serves 15.

SUSIE ROWLAND

DESSERTS

ITALIAN CREAM CAKE

CAKE
2 cups cake flour
1 teaspoon baking soda
1/2 cup (1 stick) margarine, softened
1/2 cup shortening
2 cups granulated sugar
5 egg yolks
1 cup buttermilk
1 teaspoon vanilla extract
1 (3-ounce) can flaked coconut
1 cup chopped pecans
5 egg whites

FROSTING
8 ounces cream cheese, softened
1/4 cup (1/2 stick) margarine, softened
1 (16-ounce) package confectioners' sugar
1 teaspoon vanilla extract
Chopped pecans

For the cake, sift the flour and baking soda together. Beat the margarine and shortening in a bowl until light and fluffy. Beat in the sugar. Add the egg yolks, one at a time, beating well after each addition. Beat in the dry ingredients alternately with the buttermilk. Stir in the vanilla, coconut and pecans. Beat the egg whites in a bowl until stiff. Fold into the batter. Pour into three greased and floured 8-inch cake pans. Bake at 350 degrees for 25 minutes or until the cakes test done. Cool in the pans for 10 minutes. Remove to a wire rack to cool completely.

For the frosting, beat the cream cheese and margarine in a bowl until light and fluffy. Add the confectioners' sugar and vanilla and beat until smooth. Place one cake layer on a serving plate. Spread the top with frosting and sprinkle with chopped pecans. Repeat with the remaining cake layers, frosting and chopped pecans. Serves 12.

SABRA RODGERS, *President 2004–2005*

DESSERTS

IRISH WHISKEY CAKE

CAKE
1 cup chopped pecans or walnuts
1 (2-layer) package yellow cake mix
1 (3-ounce) package vanilla instant pudding mix
4 eggs
1 envelope whipped topping mix
1/2 cup water
1/2 cup (1 stick) butter, softened
2/3 cup Irish whiskey

GLAZE
1/2 cup (1 stick) butter
1 cup sugar
2/3 cup Irish whiskey

For the cake, sprinkle the pecans over the bottom of a bundt pan coated with nonstick cooking spray. Combine the cake mix, pudding mix, eggs, whipped topping mix, water, butter and whiskey in a bowl and beat well. Pour into the prepared pan. Bake at 325 degrees for 1 to 1 1/2 hours or until a wooden pick inserted in the center comes out clean. Remove to a wire rack and let cool completely. Invert onto a serving plate.

For the glaze, melt the butter in a saucepan. Stir in the sugar and whiskey. Bring to a boil and boil for 5 minutes, stirring constantly. Remove from the heat and let cool for 15 minutes. Drizzle over the cake. Serves 16.

THERESA GESSER

DESSERTS

BIRTHDAY ICING

1 (16-ounce) package
   confectioners' sugar
1 cup shortening

1 tablespoon milk
1 teaspoon vanilla extract
5 to 6 drops food color

Beat the confectioners' sugar, shortening, milk, vanilla and food color in a bowl with an electric mixer at low speed until creamy. Use to frost a cake or cookies. Makes about 2 cups.

JENNIFER KUSTA

CHEESECAKE COOKIES

3 ounces cream cheese,
   softened
1/2 cup (1 stick) butter, melted
1 cup granulated sugar

1 cup all-purpose flour
1/2 cup chopped pecans
Confectioners' sugar

Beat the cream cheese and melted butter in a bowl until smooth. Add the granulated sugar and beat until light and fluffy. Beat in the flour. Stir in the pecans. Drop by teaspoonfuls onto an ungreased cookie sheet. Bake at 350 degrees for 8 to 10 minutes for a chewy cookie or 11 to 13 minutes for a crisp cookie. Cool on the cookie sheet for 2 minutes. Remove to a wire rack. Sift confectioners' sugar over the warm cookies. Let cool completely. Makes 3 dozen cookies.

NOTE: *This recipe can easily be doubled and these cookies freeze well.*

TOOTSIE CHANDLER, *Senior Sustainer*

TOFFEE COOKIES

2 1/4 cups all-purpose flour
1 teaspoon baking soda
1 teaspoon salt
1 cup (2 sticks) butter, softened
3/4 cup packed brown sugar
3/4 cup granulated sugar
1 teaspoon vanilla extract
2 eggs
1 (10-ounce) package toffee bits
1 cup chopped walnuts or pecans (optional)

Mix the flour, baking soda and salt together. Beat the butter, brown sugar, granulated sugar and vanilla in a bowl until creamy. Add the eggs, one at a time, beating well after each addition. Beat in the dry ingredients gradually. Stir in the toffee bits and nuts. Drop by small rounded balls onto an ungreased cookie sheet. Bake at 350 degrees for 9 minutes or until golden brown. Cool on the cookie sheet for 2 minutes. Remove to a wire rack to cool completely.
Makes about 5 dozen cookies.

TRACI ALLEN, *Senior Sustainer*

DESSERTS

DOUBLE CHOCOLATE COOKIE BARS

2 cups finely crushed chocolate sandwich cookies
   (about 28 cookies)
1/4 cup (1/2 stick) margarine, melted
1 cup (6 ounces) milk chocolate chips
1 (14-ounce) can sweetened condensed milk
1 teaspoon vanilla extract
1 cup chopped nuts
1 cup (6 ounces) milk chocolate chips

Combine the crushed cookies and melted margarine in a bowl and mix until crumbly. Press over the bottom of a lightly greased 9×13-inch baking pan. Combine 1 cup chocolate chips, the sweetened condensed milk and vanilla in a saucepan. Cook over medium heat until melted and smooth, stirring frequently. Pour evenly over the prepared crust. Sprinkle with the nuts and 1 cup chocolate chips. Bake at 350 degrees for 20 minutes or until set. Remove to a wire rack to cool completely. Chill, if desired. Cut into bars. Store in an airtight container at room temperature. Makes 5 dozen bars.

PAIGE LEE, *Senior Sustainer*

DESSERTS

PEANUT BUTTER BALLS

1 cup (2 sticks) butter, softened
1 1/2 cups peanut butter
1 1/3 cups graham cracker crumbs
1 (16-ounce) package confectioners' sugar
1 teaspoon vanilla extract
2 cups (12 ounces) semisweet chocolate chips
2 ounces paraffin

Beat the butter and peanut butter in a bowl until smooth. Add the graham cracker crumbs, confectioners' sugar and vanilla and mix well. Chill until firm. Shape into balls.

Melt the chocolate chips and paraffin in the top of a double boiler over simmering water or in a saucepan over low heat, stirring occasionally. Coat the peanut butter balls in the chocolate mixture and place on waxed paper. Let stand until firm. Store in an airtight container. Makes 3 to 4 dozen peanut butter balls.

GWEN VINZANT, *Senior Sustainer*

DESSERTS

WHITE FUDGE

2 cups sugar
1/2 cup sour cream
1/3 cup light corn syrup
2 tablespoons butter
1/4 teaspoon salt
2 teaspoons vanilla, rum or brandy extract
1/4 cup quartered candied cherries
1 cup coarsely chopped walnuts

Combine the sugar, sour cream, corn syrup, butter and salt in a heavy 2-quart saucepan. Bring to a boil over low heat, stirring until the sugar is dissolved. Cook over medium heat to 236 degrees on a candy thermometer, soft-ball stage; do not stir. Remove from the heat. Let stand for 15 minutes; do not stir. Add the vanilla. Beat for 8 to 10 minutes or until the mixture is no longer glossy. Stir in the cherries and walnuts. Pour immediately into a greased 8×8-inch baking pan. Let cool completely. Cut into squares.
Makes 1 1/2 pounds fudge.

ELIZABETH PATTON

PAST PRESIDENTS

Mrs. Howell C. Cobb, Jr.
1959–1961

Mrs. John Tyson, III
1961–1962

Mrs. Fritz Woehle
1962–1963

Mrs. Jimmy Cox
1963–1964

Mrs. William M. Acker, Jr.
1964–1965

Mrs. Charles A. Moss, Jr.
1965–1966

Mrs. Grantland Rice, II
1966–1967

Mrs. Jack F. Anderson
1967–1968

Mrs. Nancy H. Wagnon
1968–1969

Mrs. Sam L. Horton, Jr.
1969–1970

Mrs. Richard Bruhn
1970–1971

Mrs. James L. North
1971–1972

Mrs. A. Winston Porter
1972–1973

Mrs. Walter Whitehurst
1973–1975

Mrs. Nancy Powell
1975–1976

Mrs. Thomas F. Talbot
1976–1977

Mrs. W. Carvel Woodall
1977–1978

Mrs. Pryor A. Williams, Jr.
1978–1979

Mrs. Pete McCarn
1979–1980

Mrs. John McMahon, Jr.
1980–1981

Mrs. Roger D. Meadows
1981–1982

Mrs. Joe Calamusa, III
1982–1983

Mrs. C. Thomas Scarbrough
1983–1984

Mrs. Libby M. Brasfield
1984–1985

Mrs. Thomas A. Staner
1985–1986

Mrs. Steven Dorough
1986–1987

Mrs. Spencer Bachus
1987–1988

Mrs. Michael Padalino
1988–1989

Mrs. Gary Dent
1989–1990

Mrs. Greg Hill
1990–1991

Mrs. Fred Crum
1991–1992

Mrs. Jim House
1992–1993

Mrs. Dale Lloyd
1993–1994

Mrs. Mike Booker
1994–1995

Mrs. Richard Schoenherr
1995–1996

Mrs. Tom Sullivan
1996–1997

Mrs. Glenn Brandon
1997–1998

Mrs. Buddy Bruser
1998–1999

Mrs. Dan Moultrie
1999–2000

Mrs. William McCown
2000–2001

Mrs. Donald Morrison
2001–2002

Mrs. Jason Harkins
2002–2003

Mrs. Robert Moody
2003–2004

Mrs. Marshall Rodgers
2004–2005

Mrs. Mike Hinds
2005–2006

OFFICERS 2005–2006

PRESIDENT 2005–2006
Corinne Hinds

VICE-PRESIDENT OF FUND-RAISING
Susan Ward

VICE-PRESIDENT OF MEMBERSHIP
Susan Sturdivant

VICE-PRESIDENT OF SERVICE
Julie Woodson

VICE-PRESIDENT OF OUTREACH
Kelley Evers

TREASURER
Tyra Johnson-Pirtle

PROJECT TREASURER
Jennifer Ramonell

RECORDING SECRETARY
Dina Manly

CORRESPONDING SECRETARY
Anne Feller

HISTORIAN
Debbie Self

PARLIAMENTARIAN
Sabra Rodgers

OFFICERS 2006–2007

PRESIDENT 2006–2007
Teri Hibbard

PRESIDENT-ELECT
JoJo Stamey

VICE-PRESIDENT OF FUND-RAISING
Shari Glenn

VICE-PRESIDENT OF MEMBERSHIP
Kelley Evers

VICE-PRESIDENT OF SERVICE
Anne Feller

VICE-PRESIDENT OF OUTREACH
Julie Woodson

TREASURER
Tyra Johnson-Pirtle

PROJECT TREASURER
Kim Marek

RECORDING SECRETARY
Dina Manly

CORRESPONDING SECRETARY
Susan Sturdivant

HISTORIAN
Andrea Lucas

PARLIAMENTARIAN
Corinne Hinds

GENERAL MEMBERSHIP

Karen Allums	Anita Haywood	Robin Rich
Alexandra Allyn	Teri Hibbard	Jennifer Ricks
Julie Berthon	Corinne Hinds	Susie Rowland
Lisa Boland	Julie Huldtquist	Debbie Self
Ginny Campbell	Susan Jessup	Angie Simmons
Mary Kay Cambell	Tyra Johnson-Pirtle	Laura Simmons
Melissa Cissell	Lauren Jones	Debbie Smith
Donna Conklin	Jennifer Kusta	Meredith Stamba
Genie Crawford	Paige Lehane	JoJo Stamey
Sallie Dunphy	Andrea Lucas	Vanessa Striplin
Kelley Evers	Dina Manly	Susan Sturdivant
Lindsey Eversole	Kim Marek	Karen Taunton
Lucy Farmer	Christine Meehan	Heather Thomas
Anne Feller	Donna Moreman	Jamie Turner
Theresa Gasser	Lori Mutert	Sandy Vines
Michele Gentry	Janet Olsen	Susan Ward
Shari Glenn	Claudia Pearson	Amy Webb
Kay Goolsby	Mary Scott Pearson	Toni Wolfe
Lori Hadley	Leigh Price	Julie Woodson
Dianne Hardin	Jennifer Ramonell	Brandi Yaghmai
Bel Hart	Kris Redden	

NEW MEMBERS

Mary Brown	Ashley Hibbard	Ann Songer
Leanne Calhoun	Ramona Holly	Melissa Stewart
Saskia Cartwright	Sally McClanahan	Aimee Stone
Allison Culwell	Jennifer Montalbano	Jamie Thacker
Kimberly Dawson	Sylvion Moss	Laurie Thompson
Monica Dunaway	Elizabeth Patton	Shae Tubbs
Vicki Fancher	Jennifer Plowden	Robin Wright
Mellissa Gilbert	Andrea Reiber	
Elaine Graham	Jennifer Ross	
Julia Henderson	Sarah Schroeder	

INDEX

Accompaniments
 Black Bean Salsa, 20
 Orange Butter, 27

Almonds
 Broccoli Slaw, 47
 Chicken Breast Casserole, 95
 Connoisseur's Casserole, 64
 Crunchy Chicken Bake, 103
 Holiday Asparagus, 58
 Oriental Slaw, 48

Appetizers. *See also* Dips; Sandwiches; Spreads
 Bacon Cheese Cups, 8
 Crunchy Bread Twists, 28
 Mexican Pizza, 12
 Walnut and Blue Cheese Bites, 9

Apple
 Apple and Blue Cheese Salad, 48
 Apple Crunch, 117
 Apple Dumplings, 116
 Apple Turnovers, 117
 Cranberry Salad, 50
 Fruit and Pork Kabobs, 84

Artichokes
 Green Bean and Artichoke Casserole, 66
 Hot Feta Artichoke Dip, 17

Asparagus
 Holiday Asparagus, 58
 Marinated Asparagus, 59

Avocado
 Baked Stuffed Avocados, 60
 Best Guacamole, The, 19
 Wild Rice Chicken Salad, 40

Bacon
 Bacon Cheese Cups, 8
 Best Ever Quiche, 113
 Broccoli Cauliflower Salad, 46
 Grits and Greens, 78
 Hot Bacon and Swiss Dip, 13
 Mamaw's Hot Bacon Salad, 44
 Sour Cream Quiche, 114
 Sweet Green Beans, 65

Banana
 Banana Butterscotch Bread, 21
 Festive Banana Split Cake, 118
 Frozen Fruit Salad, 53
 Frozen Sour Cream Fruit Salad, 52
 Fruit and Pork Kabobs, 84
 Orange Creamsicle Smoothie, 30

Beans
 Baked Beans, 61
 Black Bean Salsa, 20
 Connoisseur's Casserole, 64
 Dill Green Bean Salad, 47
 Game Day Chili, 33
 Green Bean and Artichoke Casserole, 66
 Green Bean Bake, 66
 Mexican Salad, 45
 Mexican Stew, 35
 Paella, 102
 Sherry's Beef and Bean Soup, 37
 Sweet Green Beans, 65
 Tuscaloosa Chili, 32

Beef
 Beef Brisket, 87
 Beef Tips with Rice, 87
 Dried Beef Dip, 13
 Irish Stew, 35
 Sherry's Beef and Bean Soup, 37
 Steak Salad, 39
 Tempting Cheese Ball, 11

Beef, Ground
 Baked Spaghetti, 91
 Fake Lasagna, 89
 Game Day Chili, 33
 Hamburger Corn Casserole, 88
 Mexican Stew, 35
 Spaghetti Cheese Casserole, 92
 Spicy Vegetable Soup, 36
 Tuscaloosa Chili, 32

Beverages
Charity League Punch, 29
Orange Creamsicle Smoothie, 30
Wassail Bowl, 30

Breads
Beverly's Sweet Rolls, 26
Crunchy Bread Twists, 28
My Grandmother's Yeast Rolls, 27
Pecan Pie Muffins, 24
Southern Corn Bread, 25

Breads, Loaves
Banana Butterscotch Bread, 21
Cranberry Bread, 22
Holiday Pumpkin Bread, 23

Broccoli
Broccoli Caufliflower Salad, 46
Broccoli Slaw, 47
Chicken Divan, 104
Layered Broccoli Casserole, 61
Oriental Slaw, 48
Steak Salad, 39

Cakes
Birthday Icing, 131
Irish Whiskey Cake, 130
Italian Cream Cake, 129
Ooey Gooey Cake, 128

Candy
Peanut Butter Balls, 134
White Fudge, 135

Carrots
Curly "Q" Chicken Noodle Soup, 38
Irish Stew, 35
Southern Pork Roast, 82
Steak Salad, 39

Cauliflower
Broccoli Caufliflower Salad, 46
Roasted Cauliflower, 62

Chicken
Chicken and Rice Casserole, 93
Chicken Breast Casserole, 95
Chicken Divan, 104
Chicken Pecan Fettuccini, 100
Creamy Chicken Bake, 96
Crunchy Chicken Bake, 103
Curly "Q" Chicken Noodle Soup, 38
Granddaddy's Chicken, 96
Grandmother's Corn Bread Dressing, 77
King's Ranch Chicken, 97
Mexican Chile Chicken, 98
Paella, 102
Pesto Chicken, 99
Poppy Seed Chicken, 93
Red Wine Vinegar Chicken, 105
Rotel Chicken Spaghetti, 101
Savory Baked Chicken, 94
Wild Rice Chicken Salad, 40

Chili
Game Day Chili, 33
Tuscaloosa Chili, 32

Chocolate
Chocolate Chess Pie, 124
Chocolate Chip Pecan Pie, 124
Chocolate Cookie Freeze, 121
Chocolate Éclair Cake, 122
Chocolate Outrageous Pie, 125
Chocolate Peanut Butter Ice Cream, 123
Double Chocolate Cookie Bars, 133
Nut Fudge Pie, 126
Ooey Gooey Cake, 128
Peanut Butter Balls, 134

Cookies
Cheesecake Cookies, 131
Double Chocolate Cookie Bars, 133
Toffee Cookies, 132

Corn
Black Bean Salsa, 20
Connoisseur's Casserole, 64
Corn Casserole, 63
Corn Dip, 18
"Corny" Cheese Dip, 18
Creamed Corn, 62
Hamburger Corn Casserole, 88
Mama's Fried Corn, 63
Mexican Stew, 35
Sherry's Beef and Bean Soup, 37

Crab Meat
 Hot Crab Dip, 16
 Mariner Stew, 34
 Newport Crab, 109

Cranberry
 Cranberry Bread, 22
 Cranberry Salad, 50

Desserts. *See also* Cakes; Candy;
 Cookies; Pies
 Apple Crunch, 117
 Apple Dumplings, 116
 Apple Turnovers, 117
 Brown Sugar Cheesecake, 120
 Chocolate Cookie Freeze, 121
 Chocolate Éclair Cake, 122
 Chocolate Peanut Butter
  Ice Cream, 123
 Festive Banana Split Cake, 118
 White Chocolate Bread Pudding, 119

Dips
 Best Guacamole, The, 19
 Birmingham Sin, 14
 Black Bean Salsa, 20
 Corn Dip, 18
 "Corny" Cheese Dip, 18
 Dried Beef Dip, 13
 Hot Bacon and Swiss Dip, 13
 Hot Crab Dip, 16
 Hot Feta Artichoke Dip, 17
 Hot Spinach Dip, 20
 Sausage Cheese Dip, 15
 Vidalia Onion Dip, 19

Egg Dishes
 Best Ever Quiche, 113
 Sour Cream Quiche, 114
 Southwestern Egg Casserole, 114

Fish. *See also* Salmon
 Mile Marker Fish, 107
 Tuna Rice Salad, 41

Fruits. *See also* Apple; Avocado; Banana;
 Cranberry; Grape; Lemon; Orange;
 Pineapple; Salads, Fruit
 Frozen Fruit Salad, 53
 Holiday Pumpkin Bread, 23

Grains. *See also* Rice
 Grits and Greens, 78

Grape
 Awesome Grape Salad, 51
 Green Grape Salad, 51

Ham
 Birmingham Sin, 14
 Ham Delights, 54
 Sour Cream Quiche, 114

Lemon
 Crusted Fresh Lemon Blueberry
  Pie, 127
 Lemon Icebox, 126

Mushrooms
 Baked Spaghetti, 91
 Best Ever Quiche, 113
 Chicken Pecan Fettuccini, 100
 Holiday Asparagus, 58
 Irish Stew, 35
 Newport Crab, 109
 Oven Mushroom Rice, 79
 Scallops Thermidor, 110
 Shrimp Casserole, 111
 Steak Salad, 39

Nuts. *See also* Almonds; Pecans;
 Walnuts
 Banana Butterscotch Bread, 21
 Chocolate Cookie Freeze, 121
 Cranberry Salad, 50
 Double Chocolate Cookie Bars, 133
 Salmon Log, 10
 Tempting Cheese Ball, 11

Orange
 Orange Butter, 27
 Orange Creamsicle Smoothie, 30

Pasta. *See also* Salads, Pasta
 Baked Spaghetti, 91
 Baked Ziti, 113
 Chicken Pecan Fettuccini, 100
 Easy Skillet Ravioli, 112
 Fake Lasagna, 89
 Hamburger Corn Casserole, 88
 Lasagna, 90

Linguini with Pesto, 74
Macaroni and Cheese, 74
Macaroni and Cheese Casserole, 75
Pasta with Vodka Sauce, 112
Rotel Chicken Spaghetti, 101
Spaghetti Cheese Casserole, 92
Spinach-Stuffed Shells, 73
Stuffed Shells, 85
Three-Cheese Macaroni, 76

Pecans
Awesome Grape Salad, 51
Beverly's Sweet Rolls, 26
Cheesecake Cookies, 131
Chicken Pecan Fettuccini, 100
Chocolate Chip Pecan Pie, 124
Dried Beef Dip, 13
Frozen Sour Cream Fruit Salad, 52
Irish Whiskey Cake, 130
Italian Cream Cake, 129
Pecan Pie Muffins, 24
Southern Pecan Pie, 128
Sweet Potato Casserole, 70
Tuna Rice Salad, 41
Wild Rice Chicken Salad, 40

Pies
Chocolate Chess Pie, 124
Chocolate Chip Pecan Pie, 124
Chocolate Outrageous Pie, 125
Crusted Fresh Lemon Blueberry Pie, 127
Lemon Icebox, 126
Nut Fudge Pie, 126
Southern Pecan Pie, 128

Pineapple
Festive Banana Split Cake, 118
Frozen Fruit Salad, 53
Frozen Sour Cream Fruit Salad, 52

Pork. *See also* Bacon; Ham; Sausage
Fruit and Pork Kabobs, 84
Pork "Tender" Loin, 83
Southern Pork Roast, 82

Potatoes
Creamy Cheese Potatoes, 67
Garlic Mashed Potatoes, 67
Hash Brown Casserole, 69
Heavenly Cream Potato Casserole, 68
Irish Stew, 35
Potato Soup, 39
Southern Pork Roast, 82

Poultry. *See* Chicken

Quail, Marinated, 106

Rice
Beef Tips with Rice, 87
Chicken and Rice Casserole, 93
Newport Crab, 109
Oven Mushroom Rice, 79
Paella, 102
Shrimp Casserole, 111
Tuna Rice Salad, 41
Wild Rice Chicken Salad, 40

Salads
Steak Salad, 39
Tuna Rice Salad, 41
Wild Rice Chicken Salad, 40

Salads, Frozen
Frozen Fruit Salad, 53
Frozen Sour Cream Fruit Salad, 52

Salads, Fruit
Apple and Blue Cheese Salad, 48
Awesome Grape Salad, 51
Cranberry Salad, 50
Green Grape Salad, 51

Salads, Pasta
Great Pasta Salad, 43
Vermicelli Pasta Salad, 42

Salads, Vegetable
Broccoli Cauliflower Salad, 46
Broccoli Slaw, 47
Dill Green Bean Salad, 47
Mamaw's Hot Bacon Salad, 44
Mexican Salad, 45
Oriental Slaw, 48

Salmon
Roasted Salmon Steaks, 108
Salmon Log, 10

Sandwiches
    Cucumber Sandwiches, 55
    Ham Delights, 54
    Homemade Pimento Cheese, 56

Sausage
    Baked Beans, 61
    Baked Spaghetti, 91
    Breakfast Casserole, 86
    Lasagna, 90
    Sausage Cheese Dip, 15
    Stuffed Shells, 85

Scallops
    Mariner Stew, 34
    Scallops Thermidor, 110

Seafood. *See* Fish; Shellfish

Shellfish. *See* Crab Meat; Scallops; Shrimp

Shrimp
    Baked Stuffed Avocados, 60
    Paella, 102
    Shrimp Casserole, 111

Side Dishes. *See also* Grains; Pasta
    Grandmother's Corn Bread Dressing, 77

Soups. *See also* Chili; Stews
    Curly "Q" Chicken Noodle Soup, 38
    Potato Soup, 39
    Sherry's Beef and Bean Soup, 37
    Spicy Vegetable Soup, 36

Spinach
    Hot Spinach Dip, 20
    Spinach-Stuffed Shells, 73

Spreads
    Homemade Pimento Cheese, 56
    Salmon Log, 10
    Tempting Cheese Ball, 11

Squash
    Baked Vegetables, 73
    Squash á la Bama, 71
    Squash Casserole, 72

Stews
    Irish Stew, 35
    Mariner Stew, 34
    Mexican Stew, 35

Tomatoes
    Baked Spaghetti, 91
    Baked Vegetables, 73
    Best Guacamole, The, 19
    Game Day Chili, 33
    Grits and Greens, 78
    Hot Spinach Dip, 20
    Lasagna, 90
    Mexican Chile Chicken, 98
    Mexican Salad, 45
    Mexican Stew, 35
    Mile Marker Fish, 107
    Paella, 102
    Pasta with Vodka Sauce, 112
    Rotel Chicken Spaghetti, 101
    Southwestern Egg Casserole, 114
    Spaghetti Cheese Casserole, 92
    Spicy Vegetable Soup, 36
    Steak Salad, 39
    Tuscaloosa Chili, 32

Vegetables. *See also* Artichokes; Asparagus; Beans; Broccoli; Carrots; Cauliflower; Corn; Mushrooms; Potatoes; Salads, Vegetable; Spinach; Squash; Tomatoes
    Grits and Greens, 78
    Sweet Potato Casserole, 70

Walnuts
    Apple and Blue Cheese Salad, 48
    Homemade Pimento Cheese, 56
    Nut Fudge Pie, 126
    Walnut and Blue Cheese Bites, 9
    White Fudge, 135

SIGNS FROM THE SOUTH

The Charity League, Inc.
Re: Cookbook
P.O. Box 530233
Birmingham, Alabama 35253-0233
www.TheCharityLeague.org

Name

Street Address

City   State   Zip

Telephone   E-mail Address

YOUR ORDER	QTY	TOTAL
Signs from the South at $19.95 per book		$
Alabama residents add 8% sales tax		$
Shipping and handling at $3.95 per book		$
	TOTAL	$

Method of Payment: [ ] American Express   [ ] MasterCard   [ ] VISA
                     [ ] Check enclosed payable to The Charity League

Account Number   Expiration Date

Signature

Photocopies will be accepted.